"Shots Fired, Deputy Down"

by

Craig Johnson

MANUSCRIPT

13 February 2015

Shots Fired, Deputy Down

Copyright © 2015 Craig Johnson. All Rights Reserved.

No part of this book may be reproduced in any form or by any means, electronic, mechanical, digital, photocopying or recording, except for the inclusion in a review, without permission in writing from the publisher.

For legal and privacy reasons, certain names in this book have been changed. Some dramatic license has been taken in recreating dialogue in order to tell the story.

All crime scene photos are published with the permission of the San Diego Sheriff's Department.

Front cover photograph by Craig Johnson depicting a cross with attached bullet fragment he removed from his chest several weeks after the shooting.

Rear cover photograph by Jeff Hollie Photography.

Published in the USA by: Craig Johnson, you may reach him at: shots_fired_deputy_down@yahoo.com

ISBN-13: 978-1508717751

ISBN-10: 1508717753

First Edition – Printed in the United States of America

DEDICATION

Dedicated to all the men and women in law enforcement who hold the

thin blue line,

so that they may learn from our experiences and survive to get home

each night to their families,

and to my wife who tirelessly worked to save me from myself. I owe

her my life and she is my everything.

Table of Contents

Acknowledgments..5

Prologue...6

Chapter 1: Origins...7

Chapter 2: Patrolling the Mean Streets of Vista......................16

Chapter 3: The Good, the Bad, and the Ugly.........................22

Chapter 4: Specialty Assignments..40

Chapter 5: Back to Patrol in a Foreign Land..........................55

Chapter 6: The Family Circle, and Life Outside of Work...........59

Chapter 7: East County COPPS 69

Chapter 8: The Beginning of the End 72

Chapter 9: I Shot the Sheriff 79

Chapter 10: Ali's Down 92

Chapter 11: The Rescue 101

Chapter 12: Ali's Experience 109

Chapter 13: The Hospitalization 116

Chapter 14: The Recovery 132

Chapter 15: The Trip to D.C 149

Chapter 16: The Rollercoaster Ride....................................159

Chapter 17: Trial Preparation: The End is Near..................165

Chapter 18: Doctor, Doctor, Give Me the Cure!.................181

Chapter 19: The Thin Blue Line...187

Acknowledgments

Special thanks and appreciation to the San Diego Sheriff's Department; Santee Station COPPS Team; the Santee station personnel and command, the San Diego Sheriff's Command and Sheriff William Gore, and the San Diego District Attorney's office. Special thanks to Deputy Michael S. for all he did and has endured…

…and God bless and much thanks to Deputy Ali Perez for being a survivor, mentor, friend, shoulder to cry on, and an inspiration to all, for what he has been through and what he has taught me. It is my hope that one day he will tell his own story in his book as he has much more to share on this story.

Prologue

This story starts at the beginning of my career. My work for almost twenty-five years molded me into the man I am today. The story of my life—personal and professional relationships, issues and tragedies—shaped who I am today, and who I was, when a horrific attack on me and others occurred on September 25, 2012.

This book explores the incident that changed my life forever, my recovery, and the subsequent severe depression and post-traumatic stress disorder that I, and others, have gone through after the attack.

In the end, this is a story of surviving the wounds we received, which were both physical and emotional. Most have healed, but I will carry what happened to me for the rest of my life. It's about not having our names engraved on the National Peace Officer's Memorial Wall in Washington DC—because we survived!

Chapter 1: Origins

I grew up in Los Angeles County. My dad, Merrill T. Johnson, was a lieutenant in the Los Angeles Sheriff's Department. A cousin of mine was a sergeant with the same department. I grew up in a Christian household. My dad was a choir director at our church, and my mother sang in the choir. Going to church was a normal routine for me.

My parents instilled in me a strong sense of morality and respect for others. I always looked up to my father for everything that he did in his career. My dad's career in law enforcement made it a natural choice as a career for me later in life.

When I was twelve we moved to San Diego where I have lived ever since. I studied criminal justice and photography in junior college; but eventually, when I was twenty-eight, I chose a career in law enforcement. I was naturally drawn to this career because of my background, and I'd always wanted to be a cop, but I didn't act on it immediately. After going to schools and studying photography, I found out how much a struggle building a career in that field really was.

Since I had a new wife and child, I went back to the career I'd always wanted, and I've never been happier. At the sheriff's academy, I was a few years older than many of my fellow cadets.

Many young men and women start a law enforcement career at a young age, without commitments such as a family. In my opinion younger cops haven't always struggled through many life experiences yet. As a result, these law enforcement officers may not take their jobs as seriously as they might need to in the beginning. This is in part because they haven't experienced difficulties or hardships in life. This is not to say that all young law enforcement officers are like this, but it is something that I have seen. Why? Because being a cop is a hell of a lot of fun. Some of the hard realities of this career don't hit you until later in life! The younger cadets enjoyed a spontaneous life after work, with celebrations involving parties—and, in some cases, hooking up with each other both during and after the academy.

One of those hookups lasted through the academy and is still going strong after almost twenty-five years. Unfortunately, my personal life wasn't as successful. I struggled with my finances and did my best to take care of my family. I married a woman who didn't agree with my choice of career, wasn't a fan of the establishment, and hated my Christian faith. After twelve years together—eight of them married—we divorced. My unhappiness was a shroud over my career in the early years, and later it affected the way I worked with my partners and supervisors in the sheriff's department.

I was never a great student. I always wondered why I couldn't concentrate when I read. I lost myself in other thoughts while reading. During my academy days, I was an average, if not slightly above-average, student. I excelled in firearms throughout my training. Ultimately I finished at the top of my class and won a Glock pistol as the "Top Gun" when I graduated. During the academy, each shooting qualification with a handgun or shotgun is scored. (There are many "quals" during the academy.) At the end, the scores are totaled, and the highest score is awarded the "Top Gun or Top Shot" award.

At that time, after new deputies graduated from the academy, they were all assigned to the jails. The department had two job classifications they hired: detentions deputy and law enforcement deputy. I was hired and graduated as a law enforcement deputy and was sent to the Vista Jail to work in a booking and housing facility. I was relatively young—bright-eyed and bushy-tailed; as they say—and had no idea what it was like to be a "real deputy." I *thought* I did. I was very fit after losing a lot of weight and getting in shape, I was cocky (like all new deputies), and I was ready to conquer the world and kick ass!

For deputies who work in a jail, the key was to work in a booking facility, and not to work there for too long. Vista Jail was a booking facility, but I ended up working there for three long years, which was the average at that time. Working in a booking facility allows you to see the suspects as they come off the street, often under the influence of drugs and alcohol. Suspects can be combative, and deputies have to use an appropriate level of force to overcome that resistance. I did this many times during my three years in booking. It was exciting, and there were many moments of adrenaline pumping when you worked in booking and were involved in a use of force. I had to use force in the housing units as well, once when I was attacked, unprovoked, by inmates.

Working the jails exposes deputies to an environment where inmates will try to manipulate you. I learned just how far the inmates would go to smuggle drugs and contraband into the jail. The jail and its inmates are a community. There is a hierarchy, and racism is rampant among all races. Maybe you're the minority race in the tank—that is, you're not the superior number of a certain color, so you're at a distinct disadvantage. No matter what your race, you will feel that separation whether you are black, brown, white, or any other.

Inmates sometimes attack deputies. Homemade knives, known as shanks, are common among the inmates. There's also the phenomenon of "gassing" a deputy, which is when an inmate throws feces and urine at deputies when they least expect it. In their boredom, inmates will find *something* to make into a weapon. This creates a lot of danger for the deputies, who are outnumbered. Only a couple of deputies oversee a housing module, which may have two hundred inmates under their immediate control.

Pedophiles are the most hated of all inmates. If an inmate gets the chance to reap some street justice on a pedophile, he or she will do it without regard to the consequences.

For the deputies, jail shifts are long: twelve and a half hours. We worked five days on, two days off, two days on, and then five days off. We had a night shift and a day shift, and we rotated from one to the other every four months. If you've ever done shift work, you know that all of this wreaks havoc on your body. When I was working nights, if I had time off, it was difficult for me to sleep at night. To this day, sleep is something that I struggle with, and unfortunately I don't see any changes coming soon.

The long days and nights left the deputies bored on many occasions. This translated into deputies playing jokes and goofing off while on duty, which often got deputies into trouble. One guy decided to play a joke using the internal tube transfer system. The system is a pneumatic device that shoots a tube-looking case from one working station to another. The case can hold papers, reports, and documents. Well, this male deputy thought it would be funny to send a message to a female deputy who was working in a housing unit. Unfortunately, the message was a piece of paper that had human waste smeared on it. As you can imagine, the male deputy was suspended from duty for a few days. I couldn't believe that he thought this was funny, especially since he knew the recipient wouldn't take it well, but this deputy had a history of making bad jokes and poor decisions, so this was par for the course.

When my time in the jails came to an end, I was so tired of working long shifts in the jail that I just wanted to get out of there. But I did pick up some valuable skills. I learned how to talk to inmates. Dealing with their games and cons was a great learning experience for me. I learned how to speak to them like people and not as inmates. When you do this, you break down walls between the badge (placa, in Spanish slang) and the inmate (con or convict).

Later I was able to use this skill when I interrogated suspects, and especially when I worked undercover in narcotics and gangs.

There is a tradition in the jails that a deputy who is leaving to work patrol must have a going-away party. Our tradition was to throw the deputy into the pit. The "pit" was the nickname for a safety cell (padded cell) where inmates who had drugs in their system and were out of control or mentally ill would stay, naked, so they couldn't hurt themselves. When deputies were "pitted," they weren't stripped naked, but they were physically restrained in a chair with safety belts. What followed was a weird sort of celebration where their captors poured food from the jail kitchen all over them. I'm talking about pudding, Jell-O, whipped cream, water, soda, and anything you could get your hands on. This occurred while the victim (deputy) was still in uniform. Afterward, the other deputies left the honoree in the cell for at least a half hour, so that the entire team could come down and see you in your "pity" And say goodbye.

I was well aware of the tradition, and I was determined not to be the victim of this "torture." I told everyone on my team not to try it, because I was watching and would fight to the death. I told my supervisors as well. They all assured me that they would honor my request and that nothing would happen.

On my last day in the jail, I was working in the booking area. I did this so I could run out of the facility at the end of the day and avoid capture. Suddenly I heard a call from a deputy who was involved in a fight with an inmate in the lower housing unit. This was right near where I was.

Being the hard charger that I am, I ran to the rescue and jumped on top of the inmate who was fighting with the deputy. I noticed that the deputy was the same guy who'd sent the message with feces on it through the tube system. That should have been a clue, but I missed it. As soon as I jumped into the fight, deputies tackled me, handcuffed me, and placed me where I did not want to be: the padded safety cell. Oh well, I guess they liked me—or, rather, they liked doing what they did to me.

When I left the jail that day, coated in dried soda and food, I never looked back. Many deputies loved to work overtime and would go back for easy shifts in the jail to make some extra money. Although I had fun working there, and I learned a lot, I had always wanted to be a patrol deputy. After I'd finished my stint in the jails, I never went back, except to drop off prisoners whom I'd arrested.

My last day in the jail.

Chapter 2: Patrolling the Mean Streets of Vista

As a new patrol deputy, I was assigned to the Vista patrol station, which is in the northern part of San Diego County. At that time, Vista was the busiest station in the department. The Vista station handled more violent calls for service (a radio call involving a citizen who's reporting a need of some kind), robberies, homicides, rapes, auto thefts, assaults, and carjackings than any other station. In fact, the "306" beat—a beat in a geographical area on a map defined by streets and other borders, and assigned a number—in Vista was the busiest single beat in the department's area of command.

The city of Vista had a significant gang problem when I worked there. The primary local gang was the Vista Home Boys, also known as VHB. The VHB gang, which was Latino, was affiliated with a larger and much more powerful prison gang called the Mexican Mafia, also known as the EME. It's safe to say that, at the time I worked there, most of the crime that occurred in Vista was committed by members of the VHB or people who were affiliated with that gang.

Before heading out to patrol anywhere, deputies attend a two-week refresher course. After working in the jails for several years, deputies need to reinforce what they'd learned in the academy, and to bring themselves up to speed. After a deputy completes the refresher course, he or she is assigned to a field training officer (FTO) for several months. If everything goes well, then the deputy is released to patrol on his or her own. To this day, the San Diego Sheriff's Department doesn't usually have two-man patrol vehicles anywhere, unless it's a training car or a specialty assignment. The department just doesn't have the budget to assign two deputies to each car. Besides, we're the sheriff's department, and we have a saying: "One riot, one deputy." We'll handle it!

Training in Vista was known to be stressful. It sure was for me. I was given most of the significant radio calls—which was common practice for trainees—plus all of the reports that couldn't get done during a shift. It was common for me to work overtime just to get all the reports and arrests done by the end of each day. Besides, I had one FTO who loved overtime, and collected it while I did all the work! He and I are still good friends, and he knows how I felt back then.

First days in patrol.

I completed my training on time, and I was sent out on my own. My first night working patrol, with no one sitting beside me, was a scary experience. All of the training suddenly became real. The fact that I could be on my own if something critical happened made me remember that this wasn't a game. Later, when I became a FTO and training coordinator for the station, I became very familiar with the complexities of the job. It was so multifaceted that many people just couldn't handle all of the things they had to do. Many highly educated trainees—some who spoke multiple languages—couldn't handle all of the quick decisions and multifaceted details that they had to do. In my opinion, the more educated a person was in that training environment, the more I saw him or her struggle with making quick decisions and common-sense decisions.

On the job, officer safety, your survival, and your partner's survival are the top priorities. I had partners ready to assist me, but I also knew that, at any minute, something could happen, and I'd have to handle it all by myself until the cover units arrived. Those few minutes could mean the difference between life and death.

There was a deputy-involved shooting in Vista a few years before I arrived there. A deputy attempted to make a traffic stop on a known felon. The suspect pulled out a MAC-10 automatic machine pistol, riddled the patrol car with bullets, and severely injured the deputy. At that time and during my tenure there, Vista was known as the "Wild Wild West" in our department—not just because of the suspects but also because of the deputies. We took care of business, and we made sure that we went home each night to our families—so we wouldn't allow the criminals to mess with us, unless we just couldn't avoid it!

Many deputies who were going to patrol avoided the Vista station because it was known that if you didn't measure up, you could be sent back to the jails as a corrections deputy for not being able to meet standards. We followed our training manual to a T and maintained high standards. If—after a trainee was shown how to do the job and it was discussed and demonstrated to him multiple times—the deputy was unable to perform his duties, then the deputy did not meet the standard of our department training guidelines. Not everyone failed, but the station's reputation was such that many people didn't want to go to Vista and take chances.

Failure to meet standards created one big and unacceptable problem: a lack of officer safety, which is the main factor in doing this job. We believed that if the deputy wasn't safe—not if he or she couldn't write a report—then he should not do this job. The deputy would ultimately be a risk to himself and, more importantly, a risk for me and all of the other deputies we worked with. So this was not something we felt we could compromise on, and we gained a reputation because of it. Was I brash and confrontational with people whom I trained? Absolutely. To trainees whom I offended, I apologize. My goal was to give you the tools to do the job right, and to make sure that you were not going to be killed or severely injured. (None of my trainees, fortunately, met that fate.)

Chapter 3: The Good, the Bad, and the Ugly

During my tenure at the Vista station I worked in patrol for five years. In many locations—a city or a county, for example—that's not much time on patrol. In the city of Vista, working five years in patrol was like working fifteen years in other locations on our department. I experienced every possible crime and type of call that I could get as a law enforcement officer in a large metropolitan city. We had lots of SWAT incidents and officer involved shootings as well. I think it's safe to say that I saw almost *everything* anyone who works in law enforcement could see during those five years.

One of my most horrific calls was about a fifteen-year-old kid from Las Vegas. His name was Joshua Jenkins, and he was visiting his grandparents in Vista. Jenkins arrived with his adopted parents and sister. The kid had a knack for getting in trouble, and his parents were about to place him in a school for troubled teens. As you can imagine, Jenkins wasn't happy about that.

One night, Jenkins and his parents had a huge argument. He waited until everyone was asleep. He grabbed a hammer, approached his parents' bed, and bludgeoned both of them to death. Then he did the same thing to his grandparents. Later he took his sister to a store, where he bought an axe and then murdered her as well. Finally Jenkins tried to cover up his crimes by setting fire to his grandparents' condo in an attempt to burn the bodies. Then he fled.

I learned about the murders when I started my shift as the acting sergeant the next day. We got a 911 call from a clerk in an AM/PM convenience store.

"That kid?" said the clerk. "The one who killed his family? He just asked me how to get back to Las Vegas."

The clerk had watched news broadcasts on TV and recognized Jenkins. When Jenkins asked how to get to Vegas, the clerk deliberately gave the teenager bad directions. Jenkins had stolen his parent's car and slept in it all night in Vista before attempting to flee. My team was able to locate him nearby and take him into custody.

During his killing spree, Jenkins had spared the family dog, but that was all that he spared. Later that day I walked the crime scene and saw the bodies inside the condo. They were badly burned from the fire. Jenkins had stacked the bodies together in a front bedroom.

As I said, murders, shootings, and robberies happened all the time in the city of Vista. On the other hand—believe it or not—I have memories of calls that I thoroughly enjoyed and that still make me smile. Let me tell you about three of those calls.

The first incident occurred in 1997. I was working day shift and received a call. The reporting party said that someone was yelling for help from a house across the street. I arrived and heard someone calling for help, just like the caller had told me. When I walked toward the house, the voice sounded like it was coming from outside, but I couldn't tell from where.

"Where are you?" I shouted.

"I'm in the chimney!" said the voice.

The voice belonged to a Hispanic man who was locked out of the house, where he lived with an elderly man who had severe hearing loss. The housemate simply couldn't hear his friend's cries for help.

I went around the house and found the elderly man. He was watching television in a back room. He couldn't hear me through the sliding glass door, so I banged on the glass with my hand to get his attention. *BANG! BANG! BANG!* He finally looked up and saw me. He got up and slid the door open.

"Excuse me, sir," I said, "do you have a roommate?"

"Yes I do," he answered.

"Do you know where he is?"

He shook his head.

"Sir, do you mind if I come in?" I said. "I think I know where he may be."

The old man stepped out of the doorway, and I walked inside. I went to the living room and looked up the chimney. There was a man inside, all right.

Once I was done laughing—which I'm not sure the man in the chimney appreciated too much—I called for the fire department. Of course, all of my partners and my sergeant arrived to take a look. I found a ladder and got on the roof before the fire department arrived. I saw this little man, covered in soot. His shirt was missing, and he had lost his pants trying to get out of the chimney. Yeah, you heard me. The chimney ate his pants.

The fire department arrived, strung a harness around the man's arms, and pulled him out without damaging the fireplace or injuring the man.

"I was drinking a lot last night," the man explained. "I wanted to get inside the house, but my roommate couldn't hear me. So I thought I could slide down the chimney."

Interesting idea; bad execution.

On another call I met a woman who was giving birth. As a law enforcement officer, I'd attended classes for CPR and advanced first aid. All of that training did include a little about how to deliver a baby. The most important part we learned was to make sure you didn't beat

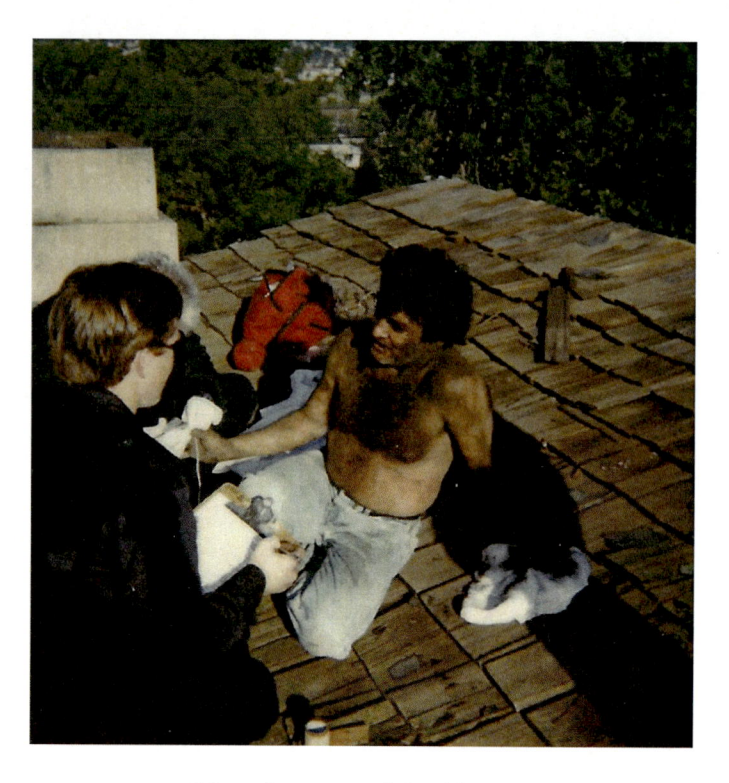

Man who was stuck in chimney.

the fire department to the call. After all, they knew how to deliver a baby much better than the deputies did.

Well, I guess the firemen and paramedics were sleeping in on the day in question. It was 1998, and one of my patrol beat partners, Todd N., (I've left out last names of deputies in light of recent anti law enforcement sentiment, to protect them) who is a dear friend, was the first to arrive at the residence. Todd was an expectant father himself, so I thought, *This is good, because he can handle this before I get there, and the fire guys will be there, and all will be well.*

Todd also had a penchant for chewing tobacco while on duty—you know, a little dip, inserted in the lower corner of your mouth. On that day, Todd arrived with a mouthful and headed upstairs to help the mother and father. No sign of the fire department yet.

Then I arrived. Still no sign of the fire guys.

"Todd?" I called out.

"Upstairs!" he replied.

I headed up the stairs and found everyone in the master bedroom. Todd and the husband were standing beside the wife, who was lying on the bed. The wife's legs were sticking up, and the baby's head was sticking out of you-know-where! Nobody was moving.

I looked at the baby. Its head was a deep blue color, meaning that it needed oxygen and had to come out, so we didn't have much time.

I looked at the husband. "Can you get me some towels, sir?"

The husband nodded and rushed out.

Todd pointed at his jaw. "Craig, I gotta go outside and get rid of this tobacco."

After Todd left the room, I was alone with the wife and the baby's head. I stepped closer to the bed and nodded at the woman. "Ma'am," I said, "the baby's head is already out. You need to start pushing."

The woman had been through pregnancy before, which was probably why this child was coming out so quickly. Unfortunately I didn't know how long she'd been sitting there with the baby sticking out. I gloved up and gently helped the baby slide out. Meanwhile, the husband returned with a stack of towels, followed by Todd. I finished bringing the baby out, and I placed it on the bed.

The baby wasn't breathing.

I tried to wake the child. No dice. I placed the baby at the mother's bosom, but that didn't work either. I was getting very nervous.

We heard sirens in the distance. *Thank God*, I thought. *The fire department will know what to do.*

"I'll bring 'em up," said Todd. He headed down the stairs.

Now what? I shrugged to myself and thought, *Oh well, Craig, just keep going!*

A few minutes passed. The paramedics dashed up the stairs. I stepped away from the bed as the medical guys took a look at the baby. They used a syringe to clear the baby's nose and mouth, and got the baby breathing.

We cops work a lot with the fire department. Many people look at the fire department as the heroes, and they often hate the cops. You can understand why: the cops take away fathers, mothers, sons, and daughters, and we put them in jail. We take kids into protective custody, and often the parents or guardians don't get them back. So on that day, it was with some pride that I was able to do something unusual. But I sure am glad that the fire guys showed up. Thanks, guys.

One more story: This one happened later that year. I was driving in my patrol car, and I was the only unit that wasn't tied up on a call or an arrest. We got a call from the southern area of Vista, which is also known as the nicest part of Vista. The neighborhoods are full of single-family homes—some very expensive, and most at an upper-middle-class level. The caller used a cell phone to call 911. The call went to the California Highway Patrol because at that time all 911 calls were initially routed to the CHP, who transferred the call to us.

"You'd better send the coroner," the caller told us.

Why? Well, the caller had taken a box cutter and slit his wrists. He was sitting in his bathtub, drinking champagne and waiting to die.

I responded and was going to wait for cover, but no one was available. Fortunately, Deputy Pete M. who was assigned to a specialty unit came up on the air. He knew I was alone without a cover unit, and answered up to cover me.

I hit the lights and siren and drove my patrol car to the caller's house. I jumped out and ran to the front door, and Pete met me at the same time. The door was slightly open.

"Sir?" I called into the house. "This is the San Diego Sheriff's Department. You called 911?"

There was silence, and then there was a weak voice from upstairs:

"You've come too soon."

I shook my head. *He means that he hasn't finished killing himself?*

I pushed the door open and headed inside. Pete followed me up the stairs. As I arrived on the second floor, the bathroom was to my immediate right. I stepped slowly to the bathroom door and saw the man sitting in the bathtub. Pete, who was behind me, was still in the hallway and couldn't see the man.

The heavyset white man, whom I believe was named Paul, had indeed cut his wrists with a box-cutter knife. As he had told the dispatcher, he was drinking champagne and was somewhat drunk.

What he *hadn't* told the dispatcher was that he had a chrome-plated .45-caliber pistol in his right hand. We later learned that Paul was a Vietnam veteran and had already shot himself once before, in the abdomen. He'd suffered from PTSD for many years.

When I came around that corner and saw the gun, the pucker factor went way up. In law enforcement, you are taught how to react to surprises. But sometimes you expect something to be a certain way, and when it isn't, it shoots off alarms in your head. On that day, my ears were ringing from those alarms. Even though cops are taught not to be complacent, we just can't predict when a routine call, such as this one, will go to shit.

"Sir," I yelled, "drop the gun!"

As I was talking, I immediately drew my handgun and pointed it directly at the man. Behind me, Pete saw what I was doing and drew his own gun.

Paul and I were just ten feet away from each other.

From the tub, Paul stared at me. He looked broken—too many nights reliving the horrors of war, too many days trying to live a normal life. He was tired, and he decided that he was out of options.

I started to talk to Paul, trying to get him to put the gun down. While I talked, I locked my gun's sights on his head, since that was the only clear shot I would have, if I had to take it.

"Sir," I repeated, "please put the gun down."

As we talked—him with a weapon pointed downward, me with my weapon pointed at him in case he decided to fire—I learned what had brought him to this point in his life.

"I can't live anymore," he told me, due to his PTSD and his never-ending memories of what he'd done in the war.

"Paul, listen to me, please," I said. "Think of your family and your friends."

"They don't matter anymore," he said. "I just can't take the pain."

"What if you prayed?"

Paul shook his head. "I don't believe in God. I'm going to shoot myself."

"Please don't," I said. "Just drop the gun."

We continued talking, but I wasn't getting anywhere with him. I tried a different approach.

"Look," I said, "if you shoot yourself, you'll permanently damage *me* as well, with the memories of this. Then I may suffer, just like you've been suffering."

Paul looked at me. Then he changed his story.

"I'm going to point this gun at you," he said. "Then you'll have to shoot me."

I tightened the grip on my gun and steadied my sights on Paul, knowing that I might have to take that shot. I continued to try to dissuade him. I told him again that if he made me shoot him, he would only make me suffer horrible memories from this incident. Time seemed to stand still, even though it had only been a few minutes. I thought about the shot. I would need to be careful of my background, and make a clean shot, so that the bullet would not travel into the house next door.

Paul and I kept talking. Finally, he looked at me and said:

"I'll…I'll put the gun down."

I didn't know if I believed him. In addition, I was standing to his left. For Paul to give up his gun and put it down, he would have to take the gun, which was in his right hand, and lay it on his left side outside the tub. When he did so, he could possibly point it at me accidentally. I was really hoping that he would follow through, but I wasn't sure how he could do it so that I wouldn't perceive it as a threat to my life. I was prepared to shoot him, and even started putting my finger on the trigger—which is something you never want to do, unless you are going to shoot immediately.

Just as I felt the trigger on the pad of my forefinger, Paul let the gun flop out of his hands and onto the bathroom floor. It clattered on the tile and lay still.

I moved into the bathroom and took the gun away. Pete came in right behind me. I checked Paul's gun. It was loaded, but he hadn't jacked a round into the chamber. If I'd had to shoot him, he would have had to pull the slide back on his .45 before firing. Which is another way of saying that I would have killed him before he could ready his weapon.

The paramedics took Paul to the hospital, where I placed a hold on him for an evaluation of his mental health. There I met his wife, who told me about his previous suicide attempts and his long history of PTSD due to the effects of the Vietnam War.

My encounter with Paul had really affected me—not because I had almost killed him, but because I felt sorry for him and wanted to help him. Months later, he contacted me and asked if he could get his gun back because he wanted to work as a security guard. We chatted for a while, and I thought that since he'd lost faith in himself, maybe he'd find it again through the church, and I encouraged him to consider it. Regarding his gun, I told him that a detective would have to make that call, but I believe he did eventually get it back.

About ten years later, Paul's wife contacted me. She thanked me for what I had done on that day, and told me she was working with a writer on a book about PTSD and suicide. She wondered if I would talk to the writer. I told her I would, and then I asked about Paul. Sadly, she told me that about a year back, Paul was finally successful in taking his life, and was now at peace. Unfortunately, I doubt that he followed my advice to reconnect with his church, and my only regret is that I didn't talk with him again, to try to help him more. But who knows if that would have made a difference?

Well, Paul, I will always remember you, and I'll always remember our encounter on that day. Looking back on that day and forward to what happened to me, the parallels were so similar. It's funny how life comes full circle.

Oh, there were many other stories. A gang member died in front of me after being shot in a drive-by shooting. There was one inmate who wrote me a thank-you letter for arresting him and changing his life; he got clean from drugs. One man inserted his head into a broken plastic injection molding machine in an attempt to fix it; the machine suddenly activated and crushed his skull. When I responded to the scene, the man was unconscious and spewing oxygenated blood out of his mouth, which looked like a Slurpee being dispensed. But the three stories I just shared with you are the ones that I will—and want to—remember, because they touched my heart in funny, good and bad ways.

I was blessed during my patrol career. I came very close to having to kill someone, but I didn't have to. I worked hard and made many arrests, which was commonplace for any good deputy who worked in Vista. My partners and I responded to countless murders, robberies, and assaults. I was involved in car chases, foot pursuits, and fights while arresting suspects, but I was never seriously injured. In 1996, I was selected as the first City of Vista Deputy of the Year by the city's crime commission.

After working as a FTO and training coordinator for Vista station, I switched over to the Community Oriented Policing and Problem Solving Unit (COPPS). What on earth is COPPS? By the sound of it, you'd think we did public relations and a bunch of community events. Well, at first, that's all the unit did. As time went on, the unit expanded its services and became a jack-of-all-trades. We did PR and community activities, sure. But we also hunted criminals, conducted surveillance, and executed search warrants. We were a busy unit. We had twelve deputies and three sergeants, but because we were "extra" deputies, we were tasked with anything that came up—things that were usually directed by the city. That's how we got our nickname: APE Squad, which stood for Acute Political Emergency Squad. Whenever the city had something come up, we had to jump to take care of it, no matter how unimportant it might be on the law enforcement spectrum. If the city that paid our salary thought it was an issue, it became one, which is completely understandable.

One of my best working relationships while in COPPS was with my partner Randy C. He is still a great friend and confidant. We worked well together, making numerous arrests and harassing the local criminal clientele every chance we got.

Randy fit me like a glove as a partner. I was always intense, and he was so calm that I think we balanced each other out. Several of our partners called us "Batman and Robin" due to our crime-fighting skills. Randy and I had some of the fun collateral duties, such as finding parolees and drug court violators. We were constantly on the hunt and arresting people. Later I changed Randy's nickname to "Superman," so he could have the respect that he deserved as my partner.

During our time in COPPS we had a serial child molester cruising the streets of Vista in his car. He kept contacting young kids and trying to lure them into his car. At one point he actually started grabbing kids and tried to kidnap a few of them by dragging them into his car. Fortunately those kids were able to escape his grasp. This dirt bag usually performed his evil deeds in the mornings as kids were going to school.

Randy and I set out on many occasions, cruising the same areas where the child molester had been spotted, hoping to spot his unusually colored sedan. Well, one day we thought we had him. We conducted a traffic stop, and sure enough, it was him! We took him back to the station and assisted the detectives with photo lineups.

During the lineups, the victims were able to identify our guy as the molester. We had enough to put him in jail. He was later convicted and was sentenced to sixty years to life. We felt really good about getting this piece of crap off the street. Randy and I would later work together again, and we remain lifelong friends.

Working patrol in Vista Ca. 1995.

Chapter 4: Specialty Assignments

After busting my ass in COPPS for four years, I was selected to work in the Special Investigations Division's (SID) Street Narcotic and Gang Detail (SNGD), again in Vista. I had proven with my hard work in COPPS that I was skilled with narcotic arrests and investigations, and I was now assigned to that area in an undercover capacity. I worked with some great partners in that unit, most importantly Keith G. He was my friend, mentor, and training officer in SNGD. He had a great talent as a narcotics and gang investigator, and did that job for two decades. In 2013, after more than thirty-three years as a sheriff's deputy, he retired. Keith loved this job more than most. Ultimately, although he had retired, he came back to work part-time with the department because of his love for the job.

Of all the jobs that I had in the sheriff's department, being a deputy in SID was the most fun, the most rewarding, and required the most work. Later I transferred to the SNGD in Encinitas, which is a coastal city in northern San Diego County. I proceeded to work both cities during different periods, and did my final four of nine years with SNGD in Encinitas.

During those years I worked with at least twenty other agencies, all of which had a similar mission:

suppression of the sale of narcotics and gangs. I made friends across the board, from local police departments (such as the San Diego Police Department, Oceanside Police Department, and Escondido Police Department, to name a few) to federal agencies such as the Federal Bureau of Investigation, Customs and Border Protection, the Drug Enforcement Agency, and the United States Marshals Service.

There are several cases that I remember fondly. While working in Vista I investigated a marijuana cultivation operation occurring in a local house. The entire house was a marijuana farm. My team, which consisted of about fourteen deputies from the Vista and San Marcos SNGDs, along with several patrol deputies, headed to the residence to execute a search warrant. After getting no response at the door, I had the door forced open by Detective Remy D. We made our dynamic entry, which is often done using force, followed by a methodical, tactically safe search of the location to prevent injuries to deputies and officers. I've conducted hundreds of search warrants using a dynamic entry and subsequent search; however, none of these were "high-risk entries," which would only be conducted by our SWAT team. Inside we were confronted by a totally naked, petite, redheaded female.

She ran to the front door and tried to open it. Needless to say, our entire team was caught off guard by that one.

She was eventually arrested along with her boyfriend for cultivating marijuana and for child endangerment. Inside the house were over 350 marijuana plants. The main water source was a 15,000-gallon water tank next to the house. That was quite an operation!

Although there was less criminal activity in Encinitas than in Vista, my partners and I, Deputies Frank S. and later Randy C. killed it on arrests and seizures. On one case, I worked with an informant who was a local drunk and addict. Half the time he was homeless. He turned me onto a suspect who was selling cocaine out of a local bar called The Kraken. Turns out the suspect had been selling cocaine out of that bar for at least six years, and law enforcement had little to no knowledge of his business. I obtained a warrant for the suspect and his residence. He was known to leave late in the morning and head to the bar. He'd stay there until the early afternoon. He sold his drugs every day—one to two ounces of cocaine every day, was what we were told.

With a search warrant in hand we waited until he left his house to make the short drive to the bar. Sure enough, the old boy, who was in his late fifties, left in his Cadillac and headed down the street. We stopped and searched him and found an ounce and a half in his pockets, all broken down to sell.

Once he was secured, we went back to his house, made entry,

and found the place unoccupied. We searched the place and found money *everywhere*. This guy was stuffing money in envelopes, furniture, safes, and dresser drawers. There was over fifty thousand dollars in cash in the house. In the trunk of the suspect's BMW we found a kilo of cocaine just sitting there. He was apparently using the trunk to spoon out his teeners (1/16th of an ounce) and eight balls (1/8th of an ounce) of cocaine to sell to his customers.

 We impounded the car, and I seized his Harley Davidson motorcycle as well. I drove that back to the station. I was wearing my TAC gear. Oh, that was a sight! I'm sure my sergeant wasn't pleased with my hopping over the speed bumps.

 Later in the week, we monitored jail phone calls for the same suspect. During one call he asked a friend and business partner to go back to the house and into the shed. Apparently, during our search we missed even *more* cocaine. So we conducted surveillance on the house, and our second suspect showed up, just as we thought he would. He left his truck and disappeared into the backyard. A few minutes later, he came back to the truck and drove away. We had a patrol deputy conduct a traffic stop on the driver for a vehicle code violation.

 Once he was out of the car, I interviewed him, searched him, and found another two ounces of cocaine in his underwear. Now as seizures go, the total amount of money and drugs we rounded up during this case was a drop in the bucket. But for a street narcotics unit, these are great seizures. Unfortunately, they also confirm a high level of drug activity in the community where we worked.

In narcotics, you work in a team environment with partners. You support them, and vice versa. My team consisted of my one partner when I was working in Encinitas, but in Vista we had the rest of our team to help us: five other detectives and a supervisor. We worked together as a team, helping each other with cases in both cities. My partner at the time in Encinitas was Frank S., a great friend and a great deputy. However, when I first met Frank, I was less than enthused. To be frank, Frank was—and still is—a big pain in the ass!

You see, in law enforcement, we see such gruesome and disgusting things that we develop a very thick skin. We have to be able to handle the things we see and do, and not take it out on our families and ourselves. To that end, we also give each other as much crap as we can, as a general rule. It's a way to blow off steam and to cope with the stress. It's funny that it also builds that team environment as well.

Frank is one of "those guys." He is, and forever will be, known as a "shit talker." On the other hand, I am well-known for the same, and I might be worse! Frank was able to get under my skin sometimes, along with his partner on the gang side, Dave B., another great deputy and detective.

So when I transferred back to Encinitas to work narcotics for the second time, I wasn't sure whether I was going to like working directly with Frank. Well, not only did we continue to talk shit about each other, but we also developed a lifetime friendship. On top of that, our work ethic was the same. We believed in the motto of "work hard, play hard." Frank and I went out and kicked ass in the coastal communities of Encinitas, Solana Beach, and Del Mar. We were so successful that our drug and monetary seizures out-totaled those of the larger, busier city of Vista, which had more law enforcement officers and detectives.

One of the best cases that Frank and I worked together was a marijuana cultivation operation in a single-family residence. An informant tip led us to this house in Solana Beach, an upscale, upper-upper-middle class neighborhood along the North County coast. This home was valued at over one million dollars. It was a two-story, 3,500-square-foot home occupied by a sixty-five-year-old white male.

Frank obtained a search warrant, and we found our suspect living in his dining room. He had a TV and a couch there. He sat, lay, and slept on that couch. He was so lazy that instead of getting up and going to the bathroom, he would just urinate into a large water bottle.

The house had been completely converted to grow marijuana. The suspect had over $500,000 in stocks, which he monitored while growing and processing marijuana. He had been doing this for over twenty years. In fact, way back then, this suspect was involved in one of the largest indoor marijuana cultivations that the sheriff's department investigated.

We ultimately seized the house, the suspect's new Mercedes SL55 convertible sports car, his Ford Thunderbird, and his truck, along with the half a million dollars in stocks, a handgun, an ounce of cocaine, and all of the marijuana.

It didn't matter what city you worked in—there were drugs and gangs. However, Vista, far and away, had more gang activity than Encinitas. In Vista, which had a predominately Latino community that used drugs, we saw a lot of heroin use. In addition, we saw heavy use of methamphetamine by all races.

By contrast, Encinitas saw more powder cocaine use among the white drug users. This was often associated with the bar scene in the community. We also saw a larger amount of marijuana being used and grown in houses and apartments in Encinitas.

Later, the abuse of prescription drugs became a very heavy problem, especially among the juveniles who lived in these areas. Kids from middle-class and wealthy families started abusing prescription drugs—probably using their parents' medications. Many drugs were used, but the drug that was used more than any other was Oxycodone, also known as OxyContin. This is a narcotic, a synthetic pain reliever. Kids found out that if they smoked it using tinfoil, the high was very much like using heroin. Of course, the kids thought that since they were only smoking it, it would be okay and not addictive. They were wrong. Some suspects we interviewed said they were smoking up to six eighty-milligram pills a day. Just one of those pills could cost anywhere from sixty to eighty dollars. To maintain their expensive habit, the kids took to doing property crimes, burglary, and auto theft. All of these crimes increased in frequency in Encinitas.

Eventually the abusers of this drug realized that heroin would give them essentially the same high at a fraction of the cost, so they began to switch.

Unfortunately, this created an even worse addiction, and the subsequent crimes continued. The problem continues to this day.

We've seen more and more youths get addicted to heroin, and we've seen an increase in deaths from overdoses.

My career in law enforcement—specifically, my work in undercover narcotics—is the reason I have such strong beliefs about and against drugs and their use, all the way down to the use of the minor drug marijuana. I am completely against the legalization of any current illegal and illicit drug. All I've seen from their use and abuse is more crime. Drug users are addicts, and they can't control their addictions. They steal and commit violent crimes to pay for their drugs because they can't hold a real job. They will do anything to make money. If they spent as much time working a real job as they did attempting to steal things such as copper wire (a current trend among drug users), they could actually do some good. But they don't want to. They want the easy way out, which is living the life of an addict, and doing whatever they have to do to make money from their crimes.

Drug use and drug users can't be regulated because they can't control their addictions. Therefore, to pay for these drugs that cost a lot of money, addicts will always commit crimes, whether drugs are legalized or not. Do you really think that making drugs legal will change anything? Will it reduce crime? If you think it will, then I have

Keith G. in ghillie suit with me on a "lay in" surveillance operation.

Me with 500 pounds of marijuana from offshore beach drop.

some beachfront property down in the desert that I'd like to sell you. Now since Proposition 47 passed, all drug possession and many other theft related crimes have become misdemeanors. This will only make crime worse in our communities, just wait and see. That's my belief, and I believe it will stand up to any argument, as far as I'm concerned. My opinion is based on a quarter century of doing this job, and seeing what drugs do to our communities and our families.

After nearly eight years of working in SNGD, and having spent my career working primarily in the North County area, I was burned

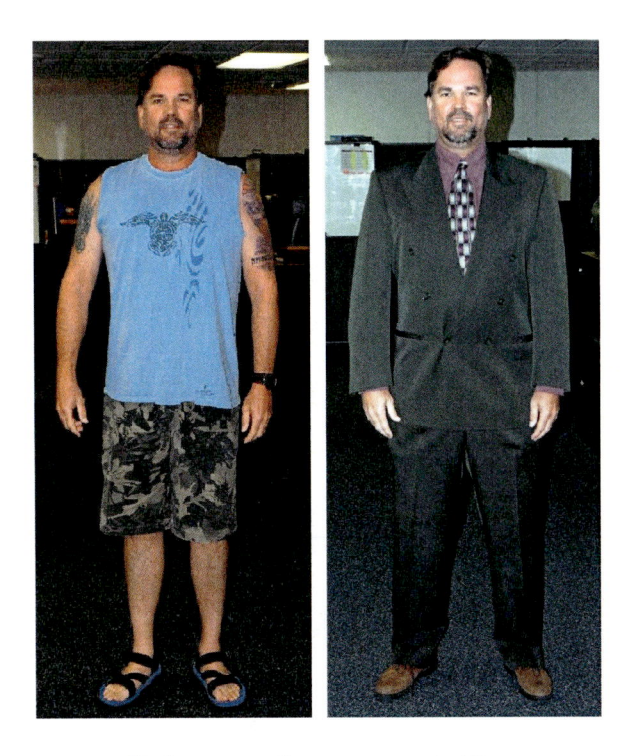

Undercover attire versus court attire.

22 foot python found under a bed during drug related search warrant.

out. I saw budget cut after budget cut affect my unit. Lack of funding crippled our efforts to combat crime, because we were the first to go. After all, patrol is the most important function in law enforcement. I understood this, but it made it impossible to do my job without a partner, which was the last straw. So I looked at moving into another position.

In addition, I was getting older and feeling the pain from years of wear and tear. My back was sore from wearing all the weight on the gun belt. My neck was sore, from being in fights and several car crashes, one of which was a pursuit of a felony suspect.

A position opened at the Federal Bureau of Investigation (FBI) Violent Crimes Task Force. I went for it. I knew from my years in SNGD that working for the feds in the DEA Task Force was fun. However, it was even more work because everything was done using the federal system, from report writing and processing of evidence, to prosecuting cases through the federal courts. Nevertheless, I was done working without a partner, and I thought the FBI job would help me get promoted to sergeant.

I landed the FBI job and began working on the Violent Crimes Task Force in the central part of San Diego. My primary function was to investigate bank robberies and crimes that had a federal nexus, such as cross-border/state kidnappings, crimes on the high seas (cruise ships), and crimes aboard aircraft—all of which are governed under federal laws. Mostly I investigated bank robberies. They were the meat and potatoes of the unit, and the most prolific crime out there.

I enjoyed working with my partners at the FBI. People who are not in law enforcement probably think highly of the feds—their name and reputation are alluring. However, people in local and state law enforcement have a much different opinion. We often see the FBI as incompetent, with no street experience—in other words, not real cops. To be frank, I was one of those people. But that was before I took a job at the FBI.

What I found at the FBI was that some of that was very true. Most of the special agents had no real law enforcement (street cop) experience. In fact, some were scientists, accountants, and all kinds of other jobs. Then they became special agents. If you work for the FBI—unless you are on a special task force that's integrated with local law enforcement—you may never be as experienced in street law enforcement as a local deputy or officer will be. On the other hand, what you *do* get in the FBI is a group of extremely intelligent people who can be great investigators in a variety of fields, some of which are far away from anything a street cop deals with.

I made some great friends at the FBI, and I cherish those relationships to this day. Like I said, the agency is admired by the public, but if people saw the ridiculous waste of paper and investigative reports that FBI personnel are required to write—which burns an inordinate amount of time—the public would see things in a different light. The agents who worked with us on the task force, and knew how local law enforcement worked, know this to be true.

Before I was transferred to the task force, I began studying for the promotion test to become a sergeant. I took these materials with me to the task force and in my down time and after work, I studied. As I said before, I had to study hard, as it has always been difficult for me to retain information. Moving to the federal task force was a calculated decision on my part. You see, our new sheriff was the former special agent in charge for the San Diego field division of the FBI.

His name was William Gore. In taking a position on the federal task force, I felt it would be a good move on my part for Sheriff Gore and his command staff to see me as not just a former narcotics investigator but also as a task force officer (TFO). Apparently it worked, because after barely a year at the task force, I was promoted to the position of Law Enforcement Sergeant in the sheriff's department. I had no idea what I was in for!

CHAPTER 5: Back to Patrol, in a Foreign Land

Once you are promoted, you move to whatever available vacancy there is, in patrol or in the courts. Sergeants no longer are sent back to the jails, but that could change in the future. That means you could be sent to North County, East County, South County, or the courts in any of those areas. Since I lived in central San Diego, it would be easy for me to work anywhere. There was no guarantee that I could return to North County, where I'd worked for over twenty-one years.

The department sent me to East County to work in the City of Santee and Lakeside county portions of San Diego County as a patrol supervisor. *East County?* What were they thinking? I knew relatively little about East County. I knew how to get there, but that was about it.

I hadn't been in patrol for over twelve years. I'd forgotten more about patrol than I remembered. Since I was approaching fifty, I had that well-known disease, "CRS." You've heard of it, haven't you? It stands for "Can't Remember Shit." The disease starts in your mid- to late forties and just gets worse as you get older.

Yes, I studied for the sergeant's test and passed, but that type of studying is somewhat robotic.

Because I'd been out of patrol for so long, I had some serious adjusting to do. A lot of my patrol skills were rusty. In addition, because I hadn't been in a patrol car in many years, I didn't know how to work the new computer very well, let alone find my way around town. To top it off, I started on night shift with little beat knowledge; and because my eyes had gotten older with age, I had to get glasses just to see the computer. My glasses had to be bifocals so I could see the road as well. Talk about officer safety issues!

The captain must have had a lot of great expectations for me, though, because they handed me the keys and said, "Here you go, and you start tomorrow night, by yourself." Oh, and one more thing: Since I had been on a federal task force, writing reports on their system, I had little knowledge of the new report-writing computer system that the sheriff's department had recently implemented, let alone how to approve and forward submitted reports.

In the end, with the help of some great deputies—Marc S., Paul B., and fellow supervisors Herb T. and Curt G.—I got up to speed really quickly. Those guys got me back into the "patrol mode" that I had worked so diligently in Vista in years past. Going back to patrol, even as a supervisor, took me back to my roots.

I worked to sharpen my skills, since it could mean the difference between life and death for me or one of my deputies if I didn't get to one of them during a time of need.

During that one-year stint in patrol, one of the most interesting incidents occurred when we had a report of a stolen vehicle that had been taken from a Lakeside residence. Knowing that a lot of stolen cars travel up the grade to the Barona Indian Reservation, where there is a casino, I decided to head that way to take a look. Well, this location is way off the beat and not regularly patrolled in the evenings on certain days. I told my deputies what I was doing, and I tried to get one of them to head my way, but they were all tied up on calls and reports.

Sure enough, I was driving toward the reservation when I spotted the stolen truck heading in the other direction. I tried to U-turn my patrol car on a busy single-lane road. I announced over the radio that I had the vehicle. My cover was ten minutes away.

As soon as I tried to catch the suspect, he took off, and it was a pursuit. Well, the guy decided to go off-roading. He cranked his steering wheel to the right, floored the accelerator, and roared into the dirt.

The suspect crashed into a hill (and into part of a fence that belonged to an Indian tribal leader), then fled on foot. I stopped my car, got out, and chased him.

When I ran by the suspect's truck, I noticed a female in the passenger seat. Not knowing if she was injured or armed, I stopped and detained her. While I did that, I lost the suspect, who ran into the hills of the Barona reservation. *Damn.*

My cover officers eventually arrived. I told them that the suspect was "in the wind." It was reiterated by my deputies that if you go up on the reservation to do any hunting, you always need to have a cover unit. I knew this, but that was my *oops* as a patrol sergeant.

After my mandatory year in patrol, I was eligible to put in for other assignments. I liked working patrol, but the long twelve-and-a-half hour shifts—with three days on and four days off, then four days on and three days off—were brutal. Wearing the ballistic vest and the equipment on my gun belt just wore me out. If I was going to survive in this job any longer, I had to get an assignment where I didn't have to wear all that equipment all of the time. So I put in for the Santee sergeant COPPS job when my predecessor got a new assignment. I got the job. It was back to COPPS for me!

CHAPTER 6: The Family Circle, and Life Outside of Work

Life in law enforcement is two-sided. You have your work and career, and you have your life away from work, with your family. In law enforcement, it's important to keep as much of your family and out-of-the-office life out of the work life, for one simple reason: it may save your life! However, this is almost impossible to do, as we are human beings, and we carry our problems to work just like anybody else.

I think that many people look at cops and see a person in a uniform, but they forget that cops are people too. We have families whom we love, financial issues to deal with, and everything that anyone else has to deal with in life. We have good days, really good days sometimes; and we have bad days, really bad days sometimes! The difference is that cops can't show that to the public. We can't let things affect us. We have to do our job with the utmost professionalism so it won't reflect on the performance of our duties. The department expects this, and the public demands it.

The problem is that this is so unrealistic. How do you shut off your emotions to do one of the hardest jobs in the world? How do you put aside the death of a family member, a divorce, the loss of a child from drugs or crime—and keep doing the job?

Well, you bury the emotions in your mind. That is one way. Or you put it in a place so deep in your mind that it stays there. This is what I've done for years. Is this a good thing? Of course not. That's why some law enforcement officers find a variety of ways to deal with it. We drink alcohol; some of us drink *lots* of alcohol. We play hard with toys like motorcycles, boats, or anything else that brings you joy outside of work and with those who are important to you. A small percentage abuse drugs both prescription and illicit, but there are only a handful of people that I've worked with that actually did that.

After all, when you deal with brutal murders, frequent deaths, destruction, child abuse, and other violent and disgusting things, they will wear on you—some worse than others. Many of us also use our faith and church to help us cope.

One of the things that is recommended—more now than in the past—is to get counseling for many of these issues. The problem? Many of us worry that if we reach out for help, we'll be reported to our departments and face employment issues. However, this has not been my experience, and I have sought help frequently for the issues in my life. An exception: If a law enforcement officer was suicidal and was threatening someone's life, then he or she would be reported to the agency, due to liability issues and the public's safety.

In my life before September 25, 2012, I had already dealt with a long list of personal issues that affected my mental state. I struggled with depression after my first marriage ended after eight years (twelve years of being together). When I met my wife, she had a son who was just under two years old. After we married, I adopted him. I realize now that I loved him more than I loved my wife. He was the glue that kept us together. During our marriage, I lost my father. I was thirty years old when he died. He was much older than most parents, and had me when he was fifty-four, in the early 1960s. Back then it was unheard of, although nowadays it's much more frequent with parents, especially with all the new medical assistance available.

When my first marriage ended, it was pretty ugly. My wife and I had not had a real marriage for some time. We lived in the same house, but we were heading in different directions. I had my conservative Christian beliefs and law enforcement friends and community. She had her new-age religion and expanding beliefs in that area. At one point she decided I should move out of the house. So I moved back into my mother's place for several months and tried to salvage a marriage that was already destined to be finished.

Eventually the marriage ended. I had to struggle through the separation and the divorce; but more importantly, I had to deal with the separation from my son. He was going to be a junior in high school and was about to move into manhood.

Declaring bankruptcy, selling our home, and moving into a studio apartment were all in my future. My ex-wife accused me of all kinds of things—mostly domestic violence. She tried to get me in trouble when I came over to the house to repair the washing machine. Thank God there was a neighbor up the street who didn't know us, and who saw the whole incident. He was able to keep me from getting arrested, by telling the truth about what happened. He heard her outlandish statements and saw her bizarre behavior.

Later, my ex-wife called my station and reported to my command that I was abusing her. She phoned them repeatedly, so that they had to conduct an investigation. She even called into the station, saying that I had threatened her when I left recorded phone messages. She thought that this would get me into more trouble. What she didn't realize was that she was seriously whacked in the head. *She* was the one who was attacking *me*. I had to go to work with scratches on my face. I tried to make excuses about cutting myself while shaving.

This behavior continued for months, and our relationship deteriorated more and more. To this day, we have little to no contact with each other, even after sixteen years apart. Due to her desire to be a victim, she took advantage of a friend's generosity and moved with my son to another state. I was really angry. I was trying to hold onto my relationship with my son, and now she was taking him away from me. Even more important, he only had two more years of high school with his friends, whom he had known since he was four! Who would do this to her child?

To say that I wouldn't wish a divorce like mine on anyone is an understatement. The only thing that saved me—and I mean truly saved me—was meeting my future wife. When I was in the midst of this horrible situation, I had a ride-along dispatcher join me for a shift one night in Vista. I hated ride-alongs, especially with dispatchers from the communications center. I just didn't want to have to babysit someone while I did my work in patrol. Hell, half the time dispatchers went on ride-alongs because they were looking for a date with a deputy. Well, guess what happened later?

So when the sergeant told this dispatcher that she was riding with me, I protested and tried to get out of it, with no luck.

Janine Pritchett headed out with me in my patrol car. I told her to stay in the car until we were safe on calls and no further assistance was needed. I showed her how to release the shotgun and fire it, if all hell broke loose. She later told me she thought this was stupid, and that I was just showing off. Years ago, in San Diego, a police officer was murdered, another was shot, and the ride-along was also shot. So I truly was thinking about her safety at that time.

During the shift, Janine and I clicked and had a great time, and I started to drop the coarse demeanor that I usually maintained as a survival mechanism. At an apartment complex—where it was mandatory to have two deputies on calls due to previous violent incidents there—we responded to a loud party call. I told Janine to stay in the car, but she'd had to stay in the car all night, so she got out and followed behind me at a safe distance. I gave up on convincing her to stay in the car, and decided to have some fun. My partner and I got ahead of her and found a closet to hide in. As she came by, we jumped out and scared her. She thought we were just being stupid, but it was fun.

As they say, time heals all wounds, and that certainly is true. Unfortunately, my relationship with my son didn't get better; it actually got worse.

Regular communication, and visits, gradually decreased. When my son went to college, he cut off almost all ties to me, and I didn't have a clue as to why. I think his mother had poisoned his mind to some degree, but I wonder if more was going on, and that was the beginning of the end of our relationship. To this day, I have little contact with him, although I continue to try.

On the other hand, my relationship with Janine became stronger over time. We've been married now for thirteen years. I love her for all she's done for me—and for saving my life—when she came into my life seventeen years ago. However, although we were in love and had a great life, there was something missing: a child. When we got married, Janine was in her mid-twenties, and I was eleven years older. We tried having a child after our first year of marriage, with no success. After a year and a half, we started seeing specialists.

We tried all of the routine things you do with infertility, and eventually we decided to try in vitro fertilization, or IVF. After two attempts, Janine became pregnant. She and I were excited, but it was short-lived. The embryo had no heartbeat. We were devastated. It's hard to put it into words.

The one thing that we wanted was a child. To be denied a child seemed so cruel. We had no idea why God had dealt us this blow. Janine and I took a break and continued to try the natural way, again with no results. We decided to attempt in vitro fertilization two more times. Our doctors volunteered their services in an effort to help us, to no avail.

A year or so later, we heard about a lawyer who did adoptions, and we paid a deposit in the hope that we could have a child in this way. As I got older, I thought a lot about my dad's age when I was born. I was concerned about being an older father, and whether birth parents would not want me to adopt their child. I don't know if this was a factor, but Janine and I were unsuccessful with adoptions, after working with two agencies.

Janine and I decided to try IVF again. Needless to say, we had to save a lot of money to pay for all of these procedures. I worked a ton of overtime. This time, Janine got pregnant again, and her numbers for the health of the pregnancy were climbing, which was a good sign. By the time we went back to the doctor, things again didn't look good again. The doctor couldn't find the baby, and there was no heartbeat. It turned out that Janine had an ectopic pregnancy. She had to take a drug to terminate the pregnancy. If she hadn't, it would have killed her.

Several days later, Janine could barely wake up, and was feeling out of it. Fortunately I didn't have to work when it happened. Because she was so drowsy, I insisted that she go to the hospital immediately. It was a good thing we did, because if she had gone back to bed, she probably would have died. The drug she took was causing her to bleed internally. If she had gone back to sleep, I would have lost the love of my life. Thank you, God, for being there on that day!

After surgery and a couple days in the hospital, Janine was sent home to rest, and she eventually went back to work. Janine was a San Diego police officer, so she had two difficult jobs: being a cop, and being married to a sheriff's deputy.

The emotional trauma and drama from experiencing these kinds of things is just awful. It's hard to describe what it's like and how it feels. Unless you've gone through this yourself, you will never be able to completely understand. If you have children, hold them close and know how lucky you are to not have had to deal with these experiences, because they change you forever!

Janine was done with IVF, and we went on with our lives. But the desire to have a child, for both of us, was so strong that we couldn't let it go. It had consumed us for our entire marriage.

It was all we knew! Several years later, I presented the issue to her again. It probably wasn't what we should have done, but it just seemed like we could try one more time. It was 2012, and we had been on this journey for ten of the eleven years of our marriage, with no success. We'd spent over $100,000 and suffered a ton of heartache and sadness. We had persevered, and we had a wonderful life with family, friends, and travel, but there was always one thing missing.

So we tried IVF again for the sixth time. The extraction of Janine's eggs was scheduled for September 27, 2012. Three days before the egg retrieval we learned Janine did not produce enough eggs and a seventh IVF cycle would be necessary. Little did I know that things would not go as planned for these last attempts. In the end, we were again unsuccessful; and we have finally, I think, moved on with our lives. We got another puppy, and maybe the adoption will come through one day. But we are happy and accept our lives, as God has a plan, even if we don't know what it is. One day in heaven we will see our lost children, and our lives will be in peace. That is what sustains us for our life here on earth, until we meet eternity.

CHAPTER 7: East County COPPS

When I took the reins as a supervisor in Santee COPPS, I was fortunate to have a smoothly running unit already. We were responsible for the city of Santee, which paid for most of our positions, and the Lakeside and El Cajon unincorporated areas within our jurisdiction. Our job was similar to what I did as a deputy in Vista. The difference? There was a greater emphasis on narcotic and gang enforcement, using informants and serving more search warrants. I was fine with this, and it was one reason that I wanted the job. My goal was to get myself back into special investigations as a supervisor, so this was the perfect way to do it.

All of the deputies assigned to the unit when I arrived were eventually able to promote to detective positions within the department. This was expected, because the COPPS position was a transitional job that gave you the opportunity to learn the skills of a detective. If you did well in COPPS, you would be selected for a permanent detective position.

When the senior deputies in COPPS got promoted, I had to take more of a hands-on approach to training the new people.

The new selections included some really great deputies: Danielle B., Jeremy S., Mike S., Steve W., Brett G., and Marc S., Marc came over from my patrol team. I knew he was an excellent deputy and the hardest worker I'd seen in a long time. They all worked hard, and I enjoyed mentoring them, even if they didn't always like it. It seems that most people in law enforcement like to think they know it all—more so with the younger generation. They just wanted to go forward and conquer, without taking the advice of others. This is haphazard, and it's one of the reasons we have supervisors to keep the checks and balances in place.

My biggest objective was to keep officer safety at the highest level. Having years of experience doing narcotic and gang investigations, I believed I was well suited to critiquing operations and giving suggestions, when appropriate, as to how to run certain details. As part of my duties I also oversaw the School Resource Officers and the Crime Prevention Unit.

Our unit was proactive, and I was very proud of that. We all worked well together, and we loved to make fun of each other. We spent time team-building one year by hiking in the hills of eastern San Diego County.

We went to a Padres game another year, and the group discovered—after imbibing much alcohol—that I had a penchant for "scissor kicks." This will remain a secret to those who were there, so let's try to keep it that way.

My deputies, inspired by their own direction and maybe some of my own, were making great arrests; seizing drugs, guns, and money; and writing and executing search warrants. We had a good reputation, not only for the amount of work we were doing but also for the quality of the investigations. Several members of the group took on a lot of responsibilities in investigations and in taking care of the city of Santee, and they excelled at it. This makes me proud, to this day, for the effort and the quality of the work that was done. Mark my words, every one of them will move on to bigger and better things due to their hard work and excellent efforts in Santee COPPS.

CHAPTER 8: The Beginning of the End

September 25, 2012, started like any other day—just like any cop who's been involved in a critical incident will probably say. I was driving to work that morning in my county vehicle. I was monitoring the sheriff's radio for Santee and Lakeside, like I did every morning. I remember hearing Deputy Michael L. say that he was returning to the station with several victims and their mother to contact the on-call child abuse detective. That was the first thing I heard about this investigation, and I wasn't really paying much attention.

I arrived at the office and took care of my usual administrative duties. It was a Tuesday, so the week was really just starting. We had one person out sick, and another on vacation, and nothing of significance was on the schedule for that day.

Later I saw Detective Ali Perez in the office. He had been interviewing the mother of two girls who had reportedly been molested by her boyfriend, Daniel Witczak, at their apartment in Lakeside. The reports of the molestation were recorded on video and still photos from the suspect's cell phone. I never saw the video or photos, and have no desire to do so, but I've been told that they are disgustingly graphic.

The mother of the victims had a previous relationship with another boyfriend or husband who had also molested her older daughter, so there were issues within this family that I will leave alone.

The mother came to the station with her children. The kids were two cute girls, ages six and eight. They stayed at the station with the front office clerks while Detective Perez conducted his investigation and interview of the mother. In child molestation cases involving young children, the initial interviews of kids is not usually conducted right away; and depending on their age and comprehension level, it may never be conducted, to avoid traumatizing the children and for other evidentiary reasons. So Ali didn't interview the two girls, and we found out later that during the molestation, they were unconscious—either asleep or drugged—so they would not have remembered anything anyway.

During the investigation, Detective Perez had the mother call the suspect using her cell phone. During the call, the suspect didn't admit to molesting her children, but he told her, "It is what it is." He told his girlfriend that he was going to sell the video and photos on the Internet for $50,000, which he would use to help the family survive.

Once Detective Perez obtained concrete probable cause to make an arrest, he wanted to move quickly before the suspect had a chance to flee. The suspect called the mother repeatedly, all morning, asking her when she was going to return home. She kept stalling to keep him on the hook and at home, where we knew he was.

At this point Ali came over to our office. He was good friends with Mike S., and he knew that we could help him move quickly to make the arrest of this piece-of-crap child molester. Now I've been involved in numerous arrests of child molesters, including one who was trying to kidnap kids in Vista years ago. In every situation I've dealt with, these suspects have been docile and compliant with law enforcement because they know we won't mess around. The reason these suspects—who are mostly males—victimize children is because they know they can get away with it with little kids. The molesters wouldn't dare attack an adult because they are too afraid of being discovered for their crimes. Plus, they are sexual deviants who are attracted to children, not adults. Nevertheless, my team knew that we needed to move quickly to apprehend this suspect. We also needed do our homework as to his other criminal history and his potential for violence.

The background check showed that the suspect had recently been arrested for minor domestic violence involving the mother of the victims. The suspect was not prosecuted due to a lack of evidence, which is common in minor battery cases. These cases are also very common in law enforcement contacts, and they don't rise to the level of concern for a deputy to consider the suspect to have a propensity for violence. Witczak had nothing else in his history that was of a serious nature.

We were also required to run a checklist of indicators that would constitute a high level of danger. The checklist included a wide variety of factors, and the suspect had none of these either. Some of these considerations are a violent criminal history, a three-strikes candidate, threats or acts of violence toward deputies or police officers, and prior arrests for possession of firearms and threats to use them.

The suspect kept calling, and we were concerned that he might flee. After doing a quick briefing with the entire team about the location of the apartment and the layout of the complex, I had two deputies Steve W. and Brett G. set up surveillance with "eyes on" the street, where they could see the suspect's second-floor apartment landing and front door.

During the surveillance, Deputies Steve W. and Brett G. spotted Witczak out on the landing, which provided access to his apartment and the adjacent apartment upstairs.

Now that we knew he was there, we didn't need to rush as much, so we discussed our plan to make the arrest.

When Detective Perez first came into the office, he approached Mike S. and the team while I was busy handling something else. I overheard their conversation and put two and two together from the call I had heard earlier that morning. Detective Perez wanted to go to the apartment, make contact with Witczak, and talk to him in a very low-key style. Detective Perez had already obtained permission from the mother to enter the apartment, and he had the key to the front door. Knowing what I did about child molesters, I was okay with the general plan, and I knew that, per our department policies, I was not required to be there.

As a general rule, I tried not to crowd my team on things that they could and wanted to do without the presence of a pesky supervisor. When I was a deputy, we never saw our supervisor. He was always in the office unless it was a hot call, and then would always be the last to arrive at the scene.

Things had changed a lot in the twenty-plus years since I first went to patrol, and supervisors were now required and encouraged to be out in the field, and more aware of what's going on. The department says it's for liability purposes, and I can see where it's justified; but as a deputy, if I could do a job and didn't need a supervisor, that was the way I liked it. I tried to do this with my team as much as possible.

In this case, I even told the team that they were not required to have me on scene, but I was going to go, so I could assist them.

I looked over the suspect's criminal history and saw nothing of concern. I looked at the photo and description of the suspect, and we brought up the aerial view of the apartment and the layout of the complex. I asked about firearms and was told that the suspect did have some guns and was a hunter, meaning he had rifles. In reality, the number of people we encounter and know have firearms is so high, that if we stopped doing our job on every call where someone owned guns to call the Special Weapons And Tactics team (SWAT), we wouldn't be able to complete our duties.

So with this knowledge, and knowing how docile child molesters have traditionally been, nothing raised any real issues for any of the team members, or me. What we didn't know was that he bordered on being a white separatist; these people are known for a propensity of violence towards law enforcement.

We knew that Witczak was anxious for his girlfriend to come home, because he continued to call her repeatedly. That was the biggest issue we saw. So our plan was simple: take the team in a low-key approach with perimeter protection in case he ran, and have enough backup so that if he put up a fight, we would be able to subdue him. We were simply going to knock on the door and make contact with him. If he didn't answer, we were going to use the door key as a last resort to gain access and arrest him. The mother and the victims were to stay at the station until we returned.

This was a mistake, and I take responsibility for it. I should have assigned a deputy to watch over her and her children. But we were short-handed, and we later learned how big a mistake this might have been!

CHAPTER 9: I Shot the Sheriff

Witczak's apartment was in a multi-building complex that had approximately a hundred apartments, along with a pool and play area. His particular apartment was in the northwest building and was the second-most northerly apartment. His front windows and door were on the east side of the building. He also had bedroom windows that faced the west. The apartment had two bedrooms, a kitchen, living area, and one bathroom.

The original plan was to approach from the south after staging at a nearby 7-Eleven. This approach would have allowed us to get on the property and approach the building without the suspect's knowledge. Unfortunately, there was confusion about this, and we ended up turning on the street in front of his west-facing windows. Surveillance had already seen him go inside the apartment, so we weren't sure if he'd spotted us. We found out later that he was well aware of our presence just before our arrival and during our approach, but not from anything we did.

We hopped in our undercover vehicles, and we also had one marked patrol vehicle. After passing the apartment, we parked at the south end of the complex to make our approach.

This area of Lakeside is known as a high-crime area, with a lot of calls for service, known gang members and drug users who lived not only in this apartment complex but also various others in the area.

As we made our way to the apartment, I had Deputy Jeremy S. and a trainee on the rear perimeter, in case the suspect tried to jump out of the second-floor rear windows. Deputies Michael L., Ali Perez, and Mike S. led the way. They were going to make the initial contact, with Deputy Danielle B. and me at the bottom of the stairs. Deputies Steve W. and Brett G. were still staged in the surveillance vehicle and could see the apartment and our approach.

As we got to the apartment, Ali, Mike L., and Mike S. headed up the stairs. Deputy Mike L. was the only deputy in a regular uniform. The rest of us wore black tactical vests over our civilian clothes. The vests, which draped over our shoulders and covered the upper torso, were labeled with a badge and wording that clearly identified us as sheriff's department personnel. We also wore our duty gun belts that had all of our usual patrol-issued equipment such as handcuffs, Taser, pepper spray, and a baton.

As Ali and Mike S. stepped up to the landing, Deputy Mike L. took up a position on the stairs about three or four steps down. Ali knocked on the door. There was no response from Witczak.

I noticed that Michael L. was not on the landing, and I wanted more of a uniformed presence near the door to the apartment. So, being the take-charge kind of guy I'm known as, I decided to step up on the landing, passing Mike L. and positioning myself next to Ali and Mike S.

We still had no answer at the door. I was standing with Ali at the front door, and Mike S. covered the only window that faced the landing. Ali knocked several more times, and I announced several times that we were with the sheriff's department. I also called the suspect by his first name, hoping to get him to come to the door:

"Daniel, this is the sheriff's department," I said. "We know that you're inside the apartment. We just want to talk to you."

Still we got no response.

The door had two locks: one on the handle, and a deadbolt. Ali pulled out the key and inserted it in the door handle. He turned the key, and it unlocked the handle. Then Ali put the key in the deadbolt, but the key wouldn't turn. It seemed to be jammed, either in the lock outside or from the inside.

We were wearing police radios, and I heard Deputy Jeremy S. come up on the radio.

"I can hear a child crying inside," he told us. "But I'm not sure where it's coming from."

This raised our level of concern. Did Witczak have a child in the apartment with him? If he did, was he molesting or hurting the child? The longer we waited, the worse it might get.

I looked at Ali.

"Do you want to kick the door open?" I said.

Ali nodded. "Yes."

At this point, Ali, Mike S., and I were still on the landing, in front of the apartment door. Two other members of our team were on the sidewalk below, looking up at us.

Ali turned around and got ready to kick down the door.

What happened next will stay in my mind, clear as day, for the rest of my life.

During my years as a law enforcement officer, I'd forced doors open, chased suspects, gotten in fights, and used the appropriate amount of force to arrest violent suspects. So breaking down a suspect's door was something we might do on any given day. In this case, the suspect was a child molester, but I wasn't much more concerned than during any other situation I'd been in numerous times. We needed to get inside, and we needed to do it right away.

Looking back at what happened next, I've gone over it a

million times, and I can't get it out of my head. I break it down into little pieces, and I think to myself, *Maybe I made a mistake at this point because I didn't assume the suspect could have been violent. Maybe I should have bumped up the rest of my team into a tactical entry team.*

You see, we were still working in a low-key atmosphere, just attempting to talk to the suspect. But when we forced the door, we essentially changed everything into a dynamic entry situation. This was also something that I had done hundreds of times in my career in Special Investigations as a deputy, and as a supervisor with my COPPS team. We had been trained annually by our SWAT team deputies. We had as much experience in executing dynamic entries—maybe more— than many other units. That's not to say that we were "operators" in a unit such as our SWAT team; rather, we did a lot of warrants in Special Investigations and COPPS, and in total we may have done more dynamic entries than most units. The SWAT guys tended to do more of the really high-risk warrants. (Of course, SWAT trained every week with different scenarios, and they are the true experts in tactics and training, so don't get your panties in a bunch, guys!)

Ali got ready to make a "mule kick" to the door. To execute a mule kick, you turn around and kick, the same way a mule does, with your back to the door. This allows the breacher (the person who forces entry) to use the maximum amount of leg power to force the door open. A mule kick is much more effective than a straight-leg kick to the door, which can cause injury if you do it wrong.

I moved toward the rear of the landing and told Mike S. to move up behind Ali. This is what we would do in a typical dynamic entry, with the supervisor at the rear. I don't know if Michael L. was still on the stairs, but if he was, he was very close to the front door.

From my position in the back part of the landing I could cover the kitchen window of the apartment. I tried to look inside. The apartment was very dark, even though it was high noon on a sunny day. I checked my watch: 12:15 p.m. That time is burned into my memory.

Ali mule-kicked the door, which blew open easily. (Ali is a big strong guy, by the way.) The door trim on the right side, where the handle and deadbolt were located, broke off the frame of the door, and the door flew open to the left. Ali turned around quickly, without exposing himself in the doorway, and stepped into the apartment.

The wall extended inside about eight feet at most. There was a TV in the corner. The apartment then turned to the right, where there was a living room and, beyond it to the right, a kitchen. There were two bedrooms to the rear, and a single bathroom to the rear and right.

As soon as Ali stepped into the apartment, I heard an extremely loud BANG, and everything went to hell.

The noise was so loud that it stunned me. A few moments later I figured out the sound had come from a large-caliber weapon. *Was that a rifle or a handgun?* I thought to myself. I saw Ali fall to the floor. They say that time slows down when you're in a shooting, and it certainly did in this situation. I keyed my radio:

"Shots fired; deputy down! Shots fired; deputy down!"

I then put out the words that I hoped never to have to say:

"11-99! 11-99!"

This is the radio code for the highest level of an officer needing help. When a cop hears this, he knows he will be responding regardless of where the incident is occurring. If there's even a chance that a law enforcement officer can assist, then he or she goes, and goes as fast and as safely as possible to get there. They say that the pucker factor goes to its highest level when you hear this. That is completely accurate.

All of this happened within seconds. Neither Mike S. nor I could see the suspect. He was hidden inside, behind the walls, like the coward and molester he was. We didn't have a clear shot to suppress his fire, and we couldn't get to Ali, who was down just inside the door. I could see Ali directly in front of me, about twenty to twenty-five feet away. I couldn't get to him without stepping in front of the suspect's weapon. Ali was lying on the ground, and I couldn't help him.

A second or two after firing the first shot, Witczak pulled the trigger again. I was lifting my weapon to point it at the doorway when I realized that I'd been hit. As I said before, when the first shots were fired I was stunned. I realize now that I was stunned because I had been shot. Although I didn't realize I had been shot, the physical reaction to being shot was that my body was stunned, and it seized my body up for several seconds. That's why I wasn't sure what had happened initially after the first shots. Yet I still didn't realize that I had been shot until I raised my gun up.

I looked down. My left forearm was split open like a baked potato. The muscle and tendons were hanging out, and a piece of my arm was missing.

I did a quick check to see if I could operate my firearm or move my hand. I apparently wasn't bleeding out from an arterial wound because blood wasn't gushing all over the place.

Later, when I reviewed the radio call (which was recorded), the only thing that anyone heard over the radio was the first time I announced, "Shots fired; deputy down." None of my other transmissions went out over the air. The rounds that hit me also severed my radio's push-to-talk (PTT), button, so nothing was working.

My radio was clipped to the front of my TAC vest, but for some reason the radio didn't get hit. Note to others: If you have the ability to move your radio to the rear, by your upper shoulder, so you can still reach it and change channels—or if you can move your radio to the side and back—do so. If you're in a shooting, once your radio communications are gone, you've got nothing if no one else is with you at that time.

The worst thing was that it took a year for me to find out this information. It wasn't until the case was going to go to trial that I realized most of my transmissions never went out. This is another thing that departments need to make sure deputies or officers have when they're involved in shootings: all of the accurate information, as soon as possible.

Stairs leading to suspect's apartment at top.

Top of landing and entrance to suspect's apartment.

Unless they'd read the reports for the Witczak case, no one would have known what I thought I had put out over the radio. So my radio was disconnected (but I was unaware of it), I'd been shot in the arm, and I thought that was all. Unfortunately, I soon realized that I'd also been shot in the side of my chest/abdomen. There I was, on the balcony, broadcasting words that no one could hear:

"I've been hit in the arm! We need a rescue team with a ballistic shield! I need another supervisor to assist with the rescue of Detective Perez!"

The ballistic shield is capable of withstanding high-powered rifle rounds. It would protect the deputies who could pull Ali out of there.

Unfortunately, none of this information went out immediately, but my guys on scene relayed everything pretty fast—possibly because they heard me saying it, and may have known that it wasn't going out.

As the supervisor, I tried to do everything I could. As I mentioned earlier, I accepted the fact that I failed to get the team into a dynamic tactical entry formation. But in the end, if I had, it's likely that more deputies, bunched together, may have been shot in the process. (This happened in Oakland, California, several years ago.) No one will ever know, but it is one of the demons that I have to live with.

Later, a search of Witczak's computer showed that he had been searching for or playing the song, "I Shot the Sheriff," written by Bob Marley. I thought this was very, very strange when I heard about it. I don't know if there was any meaning in that, but it's easy to think so.

Foot of apartment #74 where Mike S. and I ended up. That's my blood on the landing.

CHAPTER 10: Ali's Down

While all of this was happening, Ali was in a battle for his life. Witczak was using an M1 Garand military rifle. The M1 normally uses .30-06-caliber rounds, but Witczak had converted the rifle to a .308-caliber round, which was just as deadly.

Witczak's first shot hit Ali in the left bicep and traveled upward, severing an artery in Ali's shoulder area, shattering his upper arm and bones, and severing the nerves. This essentially took Ali's left arm out of the fight. Fortunately, Ali was right-handed and was able to use his handgun with one hand. After he was shot, Ali unloaded his handgun at Witczak—all sixteen rounds during different periods. At one point, Witczak retreated to the small hallway leading to the bathroom, so Ali adjusted his aim and tried to hit Witczak through the wall.

Within a minute after the gun battle began, Witczak shot Ali again. Keep in mind that Ali was no more than twenty feet away from Witczak, and may have been even closer. The second round was a direct shot into Ali's chest and abdomen. It tore through Ali's ballistic vest like butter.

The round not only broke Ali's ribs, but it also completely severed a portion of one rib (which was later removed from his body during surgery because it was no longer viable). The round also took out Ali's spleen, severed his colon, and damaged his lungs and diaphragm. The round exited Ali's body, leaving a baseball-sized hole in his back.

Ali lay there in front of me, and I could see him.

"Hold on!" I shouted to him. "We're coming for you!"

Apparently Ali was yelling that the suspect had an M1 rifle, and for us to come and get him, but I couldn't hear him. Herein lies more guilt for me to deal with. I wish that I had just run into the fire to try and get him out.

As I mentioned, I was just realizing that I hadn't just been shot in the arm, but that I had been hit in my left side as well. Since my TAC vest was black, I couldn't immediately see the blood. But as time passed, I could tell it was wet, and I knew I had been hit there as well.

The adrenaline was flowing from the moment the shots rang out, and it continued for at least fifteen minutes, maybe more. Because of the adrenaline, I never felt the round that hit me in the arm.

Nor did I feel the round that hit me in the side, which I believed was the second round that hit me. I had been stunned, though, and didn't know what exactly had occurred.

It felt like I was on the balcony forever, trying to figure out who was shooting at us. I knew that the shots were coming from inside the apartment, but I couldn't see the suspect. I had no idea where he was, so I couldn't return fire or use suppressive fire to push him back. Like I said, it seemed like a lifetime went by while I was standing there, but looking back, it was probably just a few seconds or minutes.

Once I realized what was happening, and after I broadcast that shots had been fired, I squatted to lower my body from any rounds that might keep coming. Mike Spears was with me on the landing as well, and I finally locked in on him. Because we were attempting to contact a suspect who was not known for violence against officers, and we were trying to keep this a low-level contact situation, we did not bring our own AR-15 rifles (which fire the .223 round).

Nor did we have the 12-gauge shotguns that were issued to us. Our weapons were in our vehicles. Since the front door of Witczak's apartment was right at the top of the stairs, Mike Spears and I could not move to the stairs to rescue Ali without putting ourselves in the line of fire again, nor could we get off the landing and regroup. We only had our handguns to fight back.

Since we were trapped on the landing, I had to hold out for my team to rescue not only Ali but also Mike S. and me. There was no

LOCATION OF PERSONNEL AFTER SHOTS FIRED

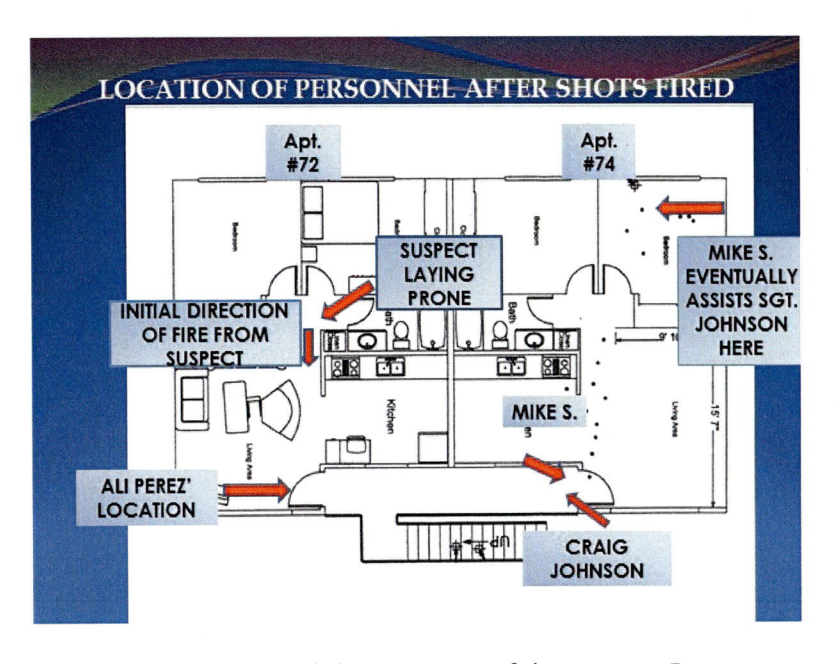

- Apt. #72
- Apt. #74
- SUSPECT LAYING PRONE
- INITIAL DIRECTION OF FIRE FROM SUSPECT
- MIKE S. EVENTUALLY ASSISTS SGT. JOHNSON HERE
- MIKE S.
- ALI PEREZ' LOCATION
- CRAIG JOHNSON

supervisor downstairs yet, and that was one of the reasons I was calling to get another supervisor on scene. I also knew that I'd been shot. I started to lose some of the adrenaline that helped me fight through the rounds that had hit me, and I was not sure how bad my injuries were. So while we hunkered down on the landing and I was putting out on the radio that we needed help, Mike S. and I gradually moved back, toward the only place we could go: the front door to the adjacent apartment.

The adjacent door was approximately twenty to twenty-five feet from Witczak's apartment door. I reached for the door handle and gave it a turn. It was locked. Shots continued to ring out from the apartment as Witczak fired at least one round at a California Highway

Round shot through wall by suspect I believe hit me.

Entrance to Apt. 72 where Ali was shot, Ali's empty gun is seen on the floor inside.

Patrol (CHP) officer who had arrived and was at the eastern end of the complex. We never figured out how many rounds Witczak fired that day, but our best estimate is eight. Initially our homicide investigators believed it was only four or five, but nobody on scene agreed, and the district attorney later felt that eight was probably correct.

I knocked on the door of the adjacent apartment. I doubted that anyone was home, but I had to try it once. No one answered the door.

Meanwhile, Witczak was trying to use the trim that Ali had broken off the door to nudge his front door closed. I was scared that if Witczak was able to close that door, then Ali was going to die. Mike S. later told me he felt the same way.

Mike and I were side-by-side at the door to the adjacent apartment. We started to put rounds into Witczak's door to keep it from closing. Ali was lying near the bottom of the door, so we kept the rounds high and above the door handle.

I was angry. I still couldn't see the suspect. I knew in general where he was, but I couldn't get a clear shot at him.

When I look back, I think that both Mike and I should have put rounds through the walls in the general area where Witczak probably was, but I don't think our rounds would have penetrated the walls, cabinets, and items in the kitchen to reach out and get him. If I had to do it again, though, I would have done that in addition to shooting at the door.

Mike and I were lucky, though, because our rounds went through the door, into the wall behind it, out the wall through the apartment and front door of the adjacent apartment, down the landing, and into the door of a third apartment, before stopping. Thankfully, no one was injured by our rounds. (This is another thing to think about, which the department teaches: watch your background for innocent people. Sometimes, however, you just don't have time.)

At this point Witczak's door was partially closed, and we still couldn't see the suspect. I started to really feel the wounds from my injuries, and I feared the worst for Ali.

While Mike and I were shooting, we were within inches of each other, and yet the rounds we fired were no louder than if we were on the range shooting with ear protection on.

In fact, we even spoke to each other, and I could hear him just fine, although I don't remember what we said.

I knew I was starting to fade from my wounds, and felt that I needed to let my team and others get to us to rescue Ali first and foremost. We had to get out of there, where we were trapped.

"Mike," I said, "kick open the door to this apartment."

When I looked in his eyes, they seemed like they were as big as quarters. I realized then that he was just as scared as I was, and I needed to get us out of there, because we were sitting ducks.

CHAPTER 11: The Rescue

Mike kicked the door open with the same mule-kick technique that Ali had used. (Mike is another big guy, and very fit; he's one of those Cross Fit coaches and fanatics.) Well, when Mike kicked the door open, he hit me in the right side of my ribs with his boot before he hit the door, and let me tell you, it hurt! It caused a huge bruise. At first I didn't realize it was from his boot, and later I thought it was from another round that had hit me but was stopped by my tactical vest.

Once the door was open, Mike helped me up, and we tactically backed ourselves into the apartment, which turned out to be vacant and empty. Mike wanted to move to the rear bedroom, farthest away from the suspect, to give us maximum protection from the rifle rounds. In my mind I was saying, *No, we need to stay at the door and coordinate Ali's rescue.* But I hesitated and let Mike get me to safety in the back bedroom. It was probably the right thing to do; but to this day, this is another factor for me that I've had to deal with.

Mike and I hunkered down in the bedroom with our eyes on the front door of the apartment we were in, just in case Witczak came through the door. We were prepared to light him up with gunfire and finish this attack, but we never got the chance.

I finally realized that my radio was not working, so I disconnected my earpiece and PTT (Push to Talk) button so I could use the radio by itself. Next door, Witczak was still firing his rifle.

The only windows we could escape through faced the west. If we went out those windows, or someone tried to get us out from the outside, they would be in the line of fire from Witczak's own windows that faced the same way. I fiddled with my radio and got it working, so I was finally able to broadcast my new location. I had the volume turned up because I had trouble hearing because the shots and yelling from deputies outside was so loud. Mike was worried that the sound of the radio would attract Witczak to our location, so he kept telling me to turn it down. I tried to, but every time I did, it was impossible to hear the radio, and I had to turn it up again. I was hoping the local patrol supervisor would get there, but he was brand new and I had little confidence that he would get there in time, or would know what to do.

Mike also got on the radio, and let everyone know we were trapped in the bedroom nearest the northwest corner of the apartment building. He advised that we didn't have a way out of the apartment without being in the line of fire. He and other deputies briefly discussed a plan to kick out the walls of the apartment on the north side, which was the only safe way to escape.

Unfortunately, to do this in a short amount of time, and without the proper tools, would be impossible. More importantly, the rescue of Ali was the most important thing, and Mike and I now had no control over that because we couldn't see into Witczak's apartment.

With that realization, I gave up trying to be in command of the situation. I was bleeding from my arm and my side, and the pain was starting to set in. I had no idea how bad the injury was to my side and chest area because the TAC vest covered everything up. There was no way in the middle of this battle that I was going to take off that vest!

I later learned what everyone else was doing to save Ali, Mike, and me. Steve W., who was "on the eye," came running out from the surveillance vehicle when he heard the shots. He ran across the lower apartments in front of the suspect's shooting platform. He was trying to get to the van in which we had transported our team. Steve wanted to get his patrol rifle, the Colt .223 high-capacity rifle. He disregarded his own safety to get to his van. He didn't have the equipment with him at the time, because he thought he would just be on surveillance.

When Steve W. ran across the complex, he fired at least four rounds towards the suspect's apartment, as suppression rounds, to protect himself. This was completely acceptable under the circumstances, but needs to be done while considering your background so you don't hit innocent bystanders.

At the same time, Jeremy S. came around from his rear perimeter position to the front of the complex. Anthony A., who was one of my school resource officers at the adjacent El Capitan High School, heard the call, locked down his campus, and was one of the first people on scene who were not with our immediate group. Along with Danielle B., Brett G., and others, everyone surrounded the apartment and started to develop a plan of rescue.

Mike and I could hear each other, and the rounds we fired sounded muffled, as if we had hearing protection on. In addition, I had tunnel vision. I was focused on the door that was open, seeing Ali, and looking for the suspect to pop his head up. I found out later from Anthony A. that the group of deputies was yelling at me, and I didn't have a clue! I didn't want to do anything except look at the door down the landing, in case Witczak came out.

So although Mike and I felt like we were all alone, in reality we had our team with us the entire time. The auditory and visual exclusionary experiences that Mike and I had are normal in shooting situations.

Once in a while I heard Jeremy S.'s voice come on the radio. Like me, he was asking for a ballistic shield to make the rescue. It was the only way we could get to Ali, handle the impact of the rounds Witczak was firing, and not get anyone killed.

While this was going on, eventually Ali somehow found the strength to push himself partially out the door of the apartment and onto the landing. Deputies Jeremy S., Anthony A., and Danielle B., along with an off-duty San Diego police officer and others, saw this and immediately moved to rescue Ali. The San Diego police officer was on his way to work and heard the radio traffic, so he responded to help out. He was also a SWAT team member for S.D.P.D., and he had compression bandages, a rifle, and training that made it great to have his assistance.

Now there is a lot of controversy among the sheriff's department members who were there as to what occurred with regard to the rescue. The department—specifically, members of our public affairs unit—touted the SDPD officer as the savior of the day. They went on camera telling the media how he came in, coordinated the rescue, and saved the day. The reality is much different.

I confirmed exactly what happened by interviewing Deputies Danielle B., Jeremy S., Anthony A., and Larry H. as to their roles in the rescue. In addition, I reviewed all the reports of deputies and everyone who was on scene. Here's how it went:

Together my deputies and the SDPD officer developed a plan to rescue Ali. They went up the landing together and worked as a team to complete the task—not by anyone's direction or orders, as some people have claimed. The SDPD officer definitely assisted as a team player with the rescue of Ali. After they got Ali down the stairs, he gave Anthony A. a compression bandage, which Anthony applied to his shoulder.

I guess the biggest reason I feel it's important to get the facts straight is that some people got all the credit for putting this rescue together and making it happen, while the truth has never been told. It was also reported that the SDPD officer escorted two children and their mother from the apartment complex, which he did, but only after other deputies (Larry H. and Jeremy S.) had gotten them out of the way of the actual gunfire.

It turned out that one of the rescuers, Deputy Larry H., was wearing an experimental lapel recording camera on his shirt, and that camera captured a lot of the rescue and arrest of the suspect. I have a copy of this video, and it clearly shows Larry H. and Jeremy S. getting the kids and their mother to safety first, and then passing them off to the S.D.P.D. officer.

It infuriated me, and many on our department, to hear on the news how a S.D.P.D. officer came in on his white shiny horse and saved the day. My deputies and others were already there, taking action and making moves to make the rescue, before he even got there. His assistance was welcome and an integral part of the team effort to rescue all of us, and I'm glad he was there. I want to set the record straight, and honor all those who did what they did. They're all heroes in my eyes, including the S.D.P.D. officer, but they all deserve the recognition of their actions, which they didn't all get on that scary day.

Based on the radio traffic, which has time-stamped entries, I estimated that this gun battle and rescue took over fifteen minutes from beginning to end, and there were at least thirty rounds fired by all those involved, maybe more. A subsequent search of Witczak's apartment revealed several rifles, hundreds of rounds of ammunition, a handgun, and various hunting gear.

Do I think he ambushed us? Yes! His girlfriend, who was instructed to stay at the station, either called him, or he called her. Either way, she answered the phone.

This was during the time that we were approaching the residence. The girlfriend later went to the scene when everything was over. She told the news media who she was, and that she could hear gunfire on her phone while she was trying to talk to Witczak. I believe that she told him we were coming, probably in a fit of rage. In any event, prior to this, I believe Witczak had planned to kill his girlfriend and was hoping she would come home to him before she notified law enforcement. We had no way of knowing this, but given that he was obviously ready for us, I believe she would have been the first victim killed, and he was either planning to shoot it out with us, or kill himself after he killed her. Witczak hasn't explained this, and he probably never will, but I believe his girlfriend told him that we were coming. He was ready to carry out the actions that he took on that day.

CHAPTER 12: Ali's Experience

As Ali lay trapped in the suspect's apartment, he experienced one of the greatest moments a human being and a Christian can have in life. Ali's account of what happened comes from the interview conducted by homicide investigators and from what Ali personally told me. There is no way I can re-tell his story and give it justice the way Ali can. I don't want to publicize this part for any other reason than to give praise to God for being there during his hour of need. Ali has much more to say on this incident, and I hope that one day he will write a book about it as well.

After he unloaded his weapon on Witczak, Ali, while lying on his back and critically injured, scrambled to find the rest of his magazines in his TAC vest. However, his vest had spun around on him when he was shot, and he couldn't find the magazines. His left arm was tossed over the back of his head as well and was completely useless. He was essentially out of ammunition, and he began to feel the severity of his wounds. It's unclear to me if this occurred before or after he was shot the second time.

At this point Ali realized he needed to slow down, so he made a conscious effort to slow his breathing. At some point he lost his grip on his handgun.

Ali knew that he had hit Witczak, because Witczak said, "Oh, shit!" three times as Ali fired at him. Witczak was later found to have three bullet wounds, two in his abdomen and one in his buttocks.

Ali started to feel himself bleeding, and knew he had bled out a lot. He knew we would come and get him, but he worried if he had enough time to get rescued before he bled out, due to the severity of his injuries. He started to lose consciousness. He could hear us calling to him and telling him that we were coming. He knew that we needed to do a tactical rescue, and that no matter what, we would be coming to get him.

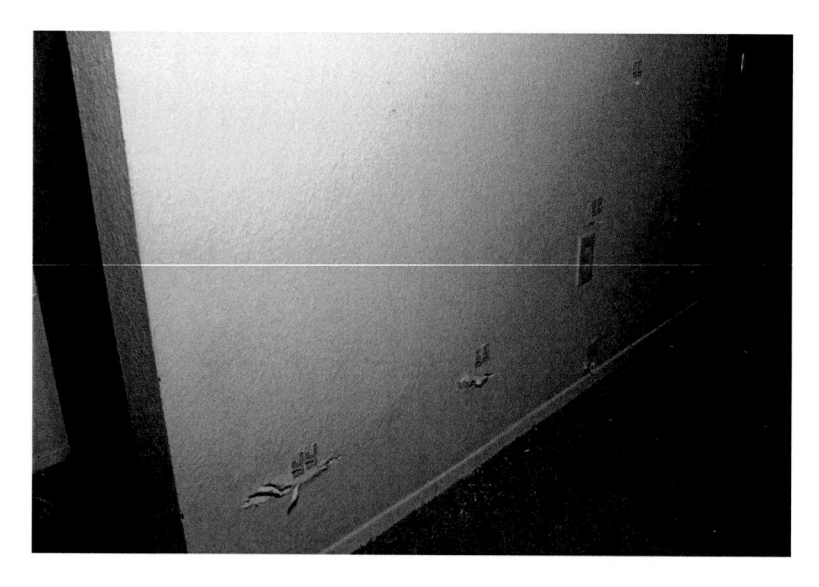

Living room wall where Ali shot rounds at the suspect, skipping several rounds into the suspect.

From across the room, Witczak called to Ali.

"Where's your sidearm?" said Witczak.

"I don't know," replied Ali. "I can't see it or feel it."

I think Witczak was asking him this because he wanted to make sure that Ali was no longer a threat to him. Only God knows why Witczak didn't kill Ali.

Later, during his interview with the homicide investigators, Ali said that he was "walking with the Lord." What he told me was that during the time after he ran out of ammunition and started to bleed out, he could see Jesus as plain as day, sitting in a beautiful chair in front of him. Ali recognized Jesus and asked the Lord a question:

"What should I do? I'm out of ammo."

Jesus didn't speak. Instead, he sent a letter or note down to Ali. It floated from Jesus' hand down to Ali, who grabbed it. The note read: I WANT YOU TO BLESS HIM.

Later, Ali left the Lord's presence and was back in the apartment.

Still lying on the floor, Ali looked over to Witczak, and saw Witczak looking back. Witczak, now had a handgun in his hand and started crawling over to Ali.

Ali thought this was it, so he told Witczak, "God bless you."

Hallway where suspect using the .308 caliber M-1 Garand rifle was lying in wait for us.

Ali told Witczak this twice as Witczak approached. This seemed to stun Witczak, who paused for a moment in silence and froze in place. Witczak then crawled up next to Ali and lay down next to him for about a half a minute.

Witczak looked at Ali and said, "I'm done fighting. I'm done." After a moment, he added, "Hey, let's go together"—meaning, *let's die together.*

Ali thought to himself, *This is it.* "I'm ready," he told Witczak. He thought to himself, *I'm already walking with the Lord. I don't want to die, and I still want to be with my family. But I accept my fate, if this is what the Lord has planned for me.*

Ali had already seen Jesus and knew how great an experience it was. He knew that he would see his family again in heaven, if this was the plan for him.

Again, Ali told Witczak, "I'm ready. I'm already with him, walking and talking with the Lord, but I'm ready to go."
Witczak again seemed stunned. "Would you like to crawl out to your friends?" he asked Ali.

"I would," Ali replied.

Witczak crawled to the back of the apartment, where the rifle was last seen near the bathroom, and allowed Ali to leave.

Ali tried the front door with his right hand. The door was closed, but the door trim prevented it from locking shut. After two tries, Ali got the door open, and crawled partway out the door.

Deputies on the outside saw a man pushing himself out of the apartment, but they couldn't tell who the man was. They yelled at him to raise his hands, but he could only raise one hand. Soon the deputies realized it was Ali. That's when Deputies Jeremy S., Anthony A., Danielle B., and the S.D.P.D. officer went up to the landing and scooped up Ali. He was hurt so badly that when they carried him down the stairs, he left a trail of blood.

Close up photo of stairs leading to suspect's apartment.

CHAPTER 13: The Hospitalization

Ali had already been scooped up and "hot-loaded" in the ambulance. ("Hot-loading" occurs when the suspect is not yet in custody and the paramedics could be in the line of fire). The ambulance roared away.

The team moved toward the suspect, who by now had also crawled out to the doorway of his apartment. The deputies secured Witczak, while simultaneously coming to rescue me. Later I watched the lapel camera that Deputy Larry H. was wearing; it showed the rescue of Ali and the subsequent arrest of Witczak. The footage was extreme and intense.

Imagine the emotions running through all the deputies and what was on their minds. I know if I was in the same position, I would be on the edge of pulling the trigger on this guy if he even flinched. They had extreme control and professionalism, and they did a great job. Having been shot three times by Ali, Witczak wasn't moving very well. So he crawled out onto the landing as well, and the deputies— slowly and methodically, in a tactical approach—took him into custody. Then they got Mike S. and me.

At first the rescuers wanted to pick me up, and I said, "No!" because I could feel the pain in my side from the bullet wound to my chest cavity. If they picked me up, it would stretch my side and really hurt.

"Just get me up," I told the team. "I can walk."

To help me walk out of there, they put my right arm over the head and shoulders of the S.D.P.D. officer. We stumbled down the stairs together and got to the next ambulance that was waiting. They also hot-loaded me. They didn't have to, because the suspect was already in custody, but they didn't know that at the time. I looked at Steve W.

"Call my wife on my phone," I said.

Since Janine was a S.D.P.D. police officer, I knew that she'd heard about the 11-99 shooting in Lakeside, and that she would immediately worry that it was me. So I wanted to call to reassure her that I was going to be okay.

"Hi," I said when she answered.

"I heard the call," she said.

"I've been shot," I told her. I heard her start to cry. "I'm gonna be okay," I added.

I wasn't sure how convincing I sounded. In any case, one of her fellow officers gave her a ride to the hospital where I was about to go.

As I said before, the paramedics didn't know that Witczak had been secured, so they hauled ass down the road to get out of there. I was barely in the gurney. I wasn't strapped in, and I tried to keep myself from falling out. Eventually, after we got out of the hot zone (area of combat), the paramedics were able to secure me.

When we arrived at the hospital, I was still conscious. Apparently the nurse in the OR (operating room) didn't realize that I had also been shot on my left side. She started to grab me right on top of the wound to push me off the gurney and onto the operating table. I screamed out, and said some kind of obscenity (I don't recall which one), and told her I had been shot there. She immediately stopped, but didn't apologize.

They put me out—under anesthesia—and I was off to la-la land. When I woke up five or six hours later, I was in the intensive care unit. A beautiful young nurse with a body that wouldn't quit was taking care of me. *Well,* I thought, *at least I am still alive.* I enjoyed the sight of the nurse for a moment. (Hey, don't be a hater! Yes, my wife already knows that I thought the nurse was beautiful. In fact, Janine made the same comments that I did.)

The doctors were able to repair the damage to my arm and stitch it closed. This left a scar on my left forearm that traveled up to the elbow. The scar was about eight inches in length, with a Y-shaped stitch at the elbow to close the gap. I had lost a part of my muscle, but I was able to move my arm and my fingers. I have damage to the ulnar nerve, which has caused permanent numbness and weakness in my arm and hand.

I was extremely fortunate, and I do believe that God was also watching over Ali and me on that day. This injury alone could have severed my nerves in my arm. Had the bullet sliced across my arm rather than up along the side, I could have lost the use of my left arm and hand. In addition, the bullet missed my arteries. If it hadn't, I would have lost a lot more blood while waiting for a rescue.

The bullet that hit my side entered my chest cavity. I didn't know this at the time. The bullet penetrated between the eighth and ninth ribs, fracturing both. It shattered into at least twenty-five fragments, some very small, and some larger. The bullet hit my colon, and the rest of the fragments went throughout my body—some toward my buttocks and some near my upper groin area—but none of them caused other significant injuries.

The injury to my colon was not severe enough to require me to have a colostomy or ileostomy bag put into place, and only needed to be stitched to be repaired. To get into my abdomen and chest, the doctors had to do what is called a laparotomy, which was a large incision in my abdomen from the bottom of my rib cage all the way down to just above my groin. They had to fish around my organs to make sure that I didn't have a bleeder from any of the bullet fragments. Again, God was watching over us: with twenty-plus fragments in my body, only my colon was injured. Unfortunately, this was not the case with Ali's injuries.

When my surgery was complete, the doctors stitched up my arm and stapled my belly. I sure wish the doctors had taken the time to stitch my belly instead, as the staples and the stretching of my skin left a huge scar that is very big in some areas, and it's disgusting to look at. Then again, I'm alive, and I really appreciate all the work that the doctors, medical staff, and paramedics did to take care of me, and especially what they did for Ali. (More about him later.)

As I said, I woke up in intensive care. I was having a very, very, bad reaction to the anesthesia. I'd always had issues with anesthesia, but because this was major surgery, and they moved all my organs around and cut my belly open, it was *really* bad.

I started to get sick. Just imagine: you've got thirty-odd staples in your gut, you've been shot in the chest and have broken ribs, your organs are sore from being shot and moved around, and now you're throwing up from the anesthesia! It sucked, and to top it off, the doctors wanted me to get out of bed within the first hour of waking up, and take a couple of steps. *Are you serious?* I thought.

My wife was in the room, as was one of my best friends, my former partner Randy C. I just kept thinking about the beautiful nurse in the room, and how I couldn't disappoint her, so I tried to walk. Man, it was one of the hardest things I've had to do in my life. I just wanted to lie in bed, but I sucked it up and was able to stand with the aid of a walker. They made me take a few steps, and that was it, thank God!

I went back to bed and vomited all night, until I got the anesthesia out of my system—or so I thought. Pain medications—Darvocet, Demerol, Dilaudid—were all in my future, and all of them made me sick. So the doctors had to give me an anti-nausea pill. At first it didn't work—until they maxed out the dosage so that I could finally stop getting sick.

After a day and a half, I was out of intensive care and in a room on the fourth floor of the hospital. Apparently the department felt that Ali and I needed armed deputies outside of our rooms for the duration of our stay, since we could no longer protect ourselves from anyone else who might want to hurt us. I thought the added security was unnecessary, but what the hell—all of the deputies got a lot of easy overtime, so I'm sure they were happy.

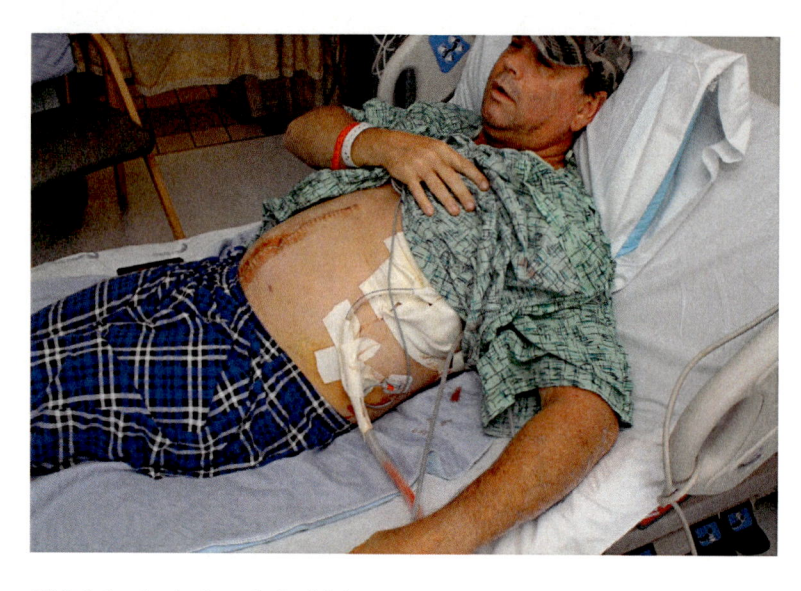

Third day in the hospital with laparotomy scar on my belly, and inserted chest tube.

Before the doctors released me to go home, my wife and I had to deal with another major issue in our lives. You see, we were still trying to have a baby, and we were involved in our sixth round of IVF treatments. Janine was taking nightly shots of hormones to grow multiple eggs in her body. Someone needed to go to our house and retrieve the shots that she was to take that night, so she wouldn't lose the eggs. Otherwise we'd have to start over and spend even more money. One of Janine's good friends got the drugs and brought them to her. Later that night, Nurse Hottie helped to administer Janine's last shot, which was called a trigger shot. This stimulated the eggs before they were extracted.

So when I came to in the hospital, I was very much aware of the need to get all this done—and the fact that, two days after the shooting, Janine would have to go into surgery to extract her eggs, or we'd lose all of them. I told her to go ahead, and she agreed.

Two days later, Janine had the procedure, while Randy C. stayed with me. Janine had a friend take her to the outpatient surgical center because she was going to be under anesthesia. Once the eggs were extracted, we had them frozen so that later we could extract more eggs during our seventh cycle of IVF, and retrieve my sperm for the insemination. This happened sometime after I was released from the hospital and had recovered—over a month later.

Unfortunately, there was only one embryo from both cycles that, once again, was not implantable due to genetic abnormalities. This dashed our final hopes for having a baby; after all we'd been through. It added to my own depression from the shooting, as well—to say nothing of how it affected Janine and her life. It seemed like everything in our lives was going wrong. Yet we still had our faith and belief that God had a plan for us. We just didn't know what that plan was, and wouldn't know it until one day we met Him and Jesus in heaven. So on we went with our lives—never quitting, just keeping on trudging through life to get to where we were supposed to go.

After four days, the doctors took the wound vacuum off my arm and examined me to see if I could be released. In addition to the injuries I mentioned above, I had a chest tube inserted that drained fluid from my lungs. I also had minor wounds on my legs that had small fragments of wood in them. I assumed that these came from the walls when Witczak fired at me, because I never saw him, and it turned out that he never saw me either.

I also had a significant wound to the left breast, near my heart. This wound was stitched, but it was a mess, and quite frankly the doctor didn't tell me what was going on with it.

Later, when the doctor removed the stitches from the still-bloody wound, it hurt like a motherfucker and put me in tears. Nor I was told I had broken ribs, until over a year later. The trauma surgeons seemed to be great, but one of the doctors had a really bad bedside manner and didn't bother to give me any real explanations about my wounds, except to say that I would be fine, and "no heavy lifting for six weeks!"

So I got out of the hospital really quickly, and I was ready to go. I hated hospitals. I spent a lot of time in them as a kid, when my dad got sick and had to have surgeries. So this was a real hang-up for me.

The department members were all over the hospital during this time, and many walked with Janine and me on the day I was released. We left through the back entrance of the hospital, trying to avoid the media circus that was all over the place. The department motor units (motorcycle cops) were kind enough to give us an escort from the hospital back to our house.

Once I got out of the car and walked inside our home, I realized how weak I was, and that this was going to be a much longer recovery than I'd anticipated. I wasn't going to jump back into work in a couple of weeks.

Ali, on the other hand, was in a much worse situation. By the time he'd arrived at the hospital, he was barely alive. He was unconscious and had little blood left in his body. The doctors immediately started transfusions, which went on for days. Ali needed so much blood that the hospital sponsored a blood drive with the Red Cross to help support him and the public in general. Deputies, administrative staff, commanders, the Sheriff himself—all gave blood for the cause. There was an amazing outpouring of love and support for both of us from the department, the law enforcement community, and especially from the general public. Folks sponsored fundraisers to help Ali and his family and me, so we could pay costs that were not covered by our insurance.

When Ali first got into the hospital, the wound to his shoulder was a major concern. He had an arterial bleed that the doctors couldn't find. He was in surgery for so long that the doctors decided to close him up to let his body recover, and kept giving him transfusions to sustain his life.

He was induced into a coma with drugs to prevent him from feeling the pain and hurting himself more. Ali was intubated for several weeks, and was in the induced coma for that long as well.

As I said before, his ribs were broken, and one had broken off inside his body. The doctors had to leave that rib there until much later, when they finally took it out. His injuries were so severe, they were concerned about any unnecessary surgery, and the rib could wait. Ali's colon was severely injured, and he had to have an ileostomy surgery, with a bag on his side to collect his human waste. He had the bag for about nine months before he had it surgically removed.

I believe it was the following day that the surgeons were able to find the arterial bleed in Ali's shoulder. His arm and bones from the elbow to his shoulder had been shattered. Eventually the doctors put a titanium rod in his arm so that his bicep and bones could heal. The fragments of bones in his upper arm and shoulder were destroyed and shattered into so many pieces. Eventually they came together and grew a mass of bone near his shoulder socket. That mass limited Ali's arm movement, and was eventually removed.

I mentioned that Witczak's second shot sent a round into Ali's chest and abdomen. The round tore through his ballistic vest like butter. The round also took out his spleen, severed his colon, damaged his lungs and diaphragm, and exited out his back, leaving a baseball-sized hole.

Ali was in intensive care for at least two weeks. He was intubated most of that time, and was under heavy medications. I regularly visited him and his family, who were basically living in the hospital waiting room. Eventually the hospital moved Ali's family to a private conference room and set it up with food, photos of Ali, and anything they could to make it a friendly place for his wife and their two kids. Sisters, brothers, aunts and uncles, his parents and his wife's parents, and their friends spent time at the hospital—it was a whole camp in there!

Meanwhile, the public, our department members, and family and friends sent cards and letters. Ali and I received so many get-well wishes—it was just amazing. The love and support from our department members was astounding. Local restaurants sponsored fundraisers, several of which I attended so I could say thanks to those who'd helped. The department put together a little photo album for us, with pictures from different units telling us to get well and be strong. This was incredibly touching. It was the idea of a friend of both Ali and me, who was a deputy herself.

I got to know Ali's family very well. Ali was still unconscious, and there were days and days of sitting around, waiting for updates on his status.

Surgery after surgery, recovery after recovery, and still he was unconscious. Ali's in-laws, brothers, and sisters basically adopted my wife and me. They were big supporters of me and my recovery, and they were big supporters of my wife Janine, who had been through the ringer as the wife of a sheriff's sergeant and as a detective with San Diego Police Department.

Our department jumped up, along with our deputy sheriff's association, to help if we needed anything, from money, to food, to clothing. Everyone was there for us—that is, except for Janine's command, most specifically her direct supervisor and the station administration. The chief showed up the first day because the media had broadcast that Janine was a police officer and that was appreciated. Many of her friends from the S.D.P.D. came to the hospital and were there for her; some even sent flowers and cards to the hospital and our house. They even offered to do errands and walk our dog.

The problem? None of Janine's station command really seemed to give a shit. Oh, they offered their support at first, but Janine worked for a supervisor who was a real jerk, especially to women who worked for him. The department turned a blind eye when it came to this supervisor, his absolute disrespect for women, and his downright abhorrent treatment of employees. In addition—unlike my command, which was there for us, checked in on us, visited us, and helped us— Janine's command simply told us, "If you need something, let us know." They never came to the hospital, never visited us at home, and I'm not sure if they even regularly called to check on Janine.

One day, Ali finally woke up in intensive care. He was no longer intubated. I finally got to see him. His brother-in-law, Sean, is another hero, in my mind. He stayed with Ali, night after night, for weeks on end. Sean is a police officer for the city of El Cajon, so he would work during the day and come to the hospital to stay with Ali every night.

When I finally got to speak with Ali, he couldn't talk, but he mouthed the words, "We got him." I started crying, and I told him, "Yeah, we sure did!"

It was at that moment when Ali first blessed me with his kindness and his caring personality, and our relationship began to grow. Before the incident, Ali and I knew about each other, but we'd never worked together because he worked mainly in East County, while I was in North County. But from that day forward, I shared a bond with him. I can truly say that what happened to Ali, how he survived, and how he witnessed to me his moments with Christ, truly saved me from taking my own life later on.

Once Ali was out of intensive care, the hospital moved him down to the fourth floor where I had been. He slowly began to recover, but got an infection and some other setbacks that hit him on his way to recovery. Janine and I visited him several times a week and spent time with him and his family.

We learned that Ali couldn't use his left arm and hand. The shooting had severed some of the nerves in his arm, and he couldn't move his hand at all. Gradually he regained some use of his hand, but at this writing he is not able to use it. For now, he cannot grip much or pick up items with his left hand, and he keeps his arm and hand in a sling most of the time.

Ali spent well over a hundred days in the hospital, and he had to come back several times for additional surgeries and to deal with complications from the surgeries. In total, Ali has had over twenty-seven surgeries, and may have to have several more in the future. We pray that he will regain use of his left hand so that he can, one day, ride motorcycles again—hopefully with me by his side.

CHAPTER 14: The Recovery

My physical wounds began to heal immediately, some quicker than the others. My abdomen was the slowest to recover, with the greatest pain and injury occurring when the doctors opened up my belly. The muscles in the stomach are very strong. It took many months for those muscles to heal after they were cut during surgery. To this day I have abdominal pain, which the doctors believe is from scar tissue and not from the fragments—all twenty-five that are still in my body. The doctors told me they routinely leave bullet fragments inside the human body because it is too dangerous to take them out; removing the fragments could cause more damage. The bullets or fragments will typically wall themselves off from your organs and protect you from further injury. It's not really a comforting thought. To this day, almost a year and a half later, I have pain in my ribs, which the doctors associate with nerve damage where the bullet fractured my ribs and may have caused long-term nerve damage.

One wound just wouldn't heal. It was the one that was on my left breast near my heart. After about six weeks, it was still bloody and wasn't healing like the rest of my wounds. So on one of my follow-up doctor appointments, I showed it to the doctor. He said that he thought I still had something in the wound, and that he would open me up if I wanted him to! I said I'd hold off and take another look at in a few days, to see how it was doing.

Well, the next morning, after my shower, I had to change my bandages, which was a daily routine by now. I examined the wound and saw that it hadn't changed. It was wet, so I began to pull at the bloody scab. You know when you have a cut or wound and you pull on it, the scab part wants to stay attached to the healing tissue? Well, this didn't do that at all. In fact, it just came out of my chest as I pulled on it, and it didn't even hurt! It was a bloody scab with something inside. I rinsed it off in the sink, and lo and behold, it was a large brass jacket piece of the bullet. The brass jacket is a softer material that is wrapped around the heavier lead bullet. The ammunition manufacturers do this, in part, so that the bullet will fragment and cause more damage to the body, while moving around the body in different areas.

I took a closer look at the fragment, which was about a half inch long and a half inch wide, but was folded in half. The fragment had the striation marks that could possibly identify it as being fired from the rifle that Witczak used. So I knew I had to turn it over to the lead homicide detective on the case. That happened to be Todd

N., who was my partner years before when we delivered the baby in Vista.

Before I did that, I took pictures of the fragment and kept them as a memento of my experience. I was also emphatic when I told Todd that I wanted the bullet back when the court trial was over. Later, it turned out that the item was not of great significance to the trial. They had pictures of it and that was apparently enough, so Todd was able to release it to me several months later. When I got it back, I already knew what I was going to do with it. I found a Christian cross to wrap the bullet around at the middle, and had it mounted onto the cross. I wear that cross every day, and will continue to do so until the day I die.

Bullet fragment I removed from my left breast.

The bullet fragment is now attached to my cross which I wear every day.

I was so glad to be alive. I had been given so much love from my coworkers, family, and friends, as well as the general public, and that made me feel great. Ali and I both received hundreds of cards and letters from the public, including schoolchildren. Several deputies asked the kids in their schools to write letters to us, thanking us for our service to the community and to get well. So many of those letters touched my heart. I framed two of them, and they hang in the office in my home. The first letter was from a girl in the fifth grade. Her name was Paulina, and here is what she said:

> Dear Deputy Johnson,
>
> Your courage is beyond us, with no measurable amount
> You go out into the world, knowing every life counts.
> You went out on that morning expecting no thanks

But you managed to show bravery that rose above

the ranks.

And I hope as you keep living, way beyond these days,

You will receive all of your deserving praise

And I hope that you are happy with, although

It may be mild,

The slightly silent, but honest praise of a child.

Love, Paulina

The second letter was from a boy named Rocio:

Dear Deputy Johnson,

I must confess that your brave deed is honorable. Not everybody has such a strong will to protect our community. What happened is of course awful, but you must know that you are a hero. Life is a valuable thing, and you risking yours for another life is something that not everybody can do, and that makes you someone other people can look up to, as well as an inspiration to others.

    I honestly want to thank you for your service and dedication. I want you to know that you have a lot of people around you who care for you and are praying for you. This period of your life may be hard, with tunnels with no way out, but I know that you will find that door with your strength and determination. It is an honor to have people like you in this world, people to look up to, people who are heroes.

Sincerely, Rocio

The sentiment in these letters really warmed my heart, and they are not just letters to me. The words ring of truth and the sentiment of children toward all law enforcement and safety personnel in this country who work each day to protect us from evil and danger. For that matter, this also rings true for all our military personnel who are in the country and abroad, working to keep this great country safe.

Later, the reality of the situation I had gone through started to set in while I was at home for three months, recovering. I dwelled on the shooting every day, throughout the day. I started to see a psychologist, which is standard procedure for anyone involved in a shooting, and especially for someone who has been shot.

So I continued on my way, healing physically while attempting to heal emotionally as well. I continued seeing my psychologist, but I was having a difficult time sleeping and I was suffering from depression. I was also seeing a psychiatrist, who prescribed medication to help me sleep and hopefully could get my head out of the depression. It seemed to work for a while, but I kept finding myself on a rollercoaster ride of highs and lows. I hated taking medication, but I reluctantly continued to do so.

I went back to work in January, just after the holidays. I had taken just over three months off to heal physically, and to try to heal emotionally.

When I went back to work, it was as a full duty sergeant. My command—specifically Captain M., Lieutenant F., and Lieutenant W.—were just as great to me as they were when I was healing at home. The department was great as well. I got regular calls from the Undersheriff, who is second in charge of the department, under the Sheriff of San Diego County. All was well with the shooting and what had happened. When the command and the department looked at what we did and how we did it, they were fine with it.

The bottom line: this is a risky job. We did our background check and quickly worked up the location, but this could have happened to a patrol deputy who might have been less equipped to deal with it. I think almost everyone with any time on will tell you that child molesters are the most docile of criminals, and that is why they victimize children. Child molesters are known to run or cower in the corner rather than assault law enforcement officers. So for Witczak to behave the way he did was regarded as an anomaly in criminal behavior. Still, it was a lesson learned; and after this, anyone going after a child molester was closely scrutinized because of that knee-jerk reaction that we in law enforcement often have. Many times, in law enforcement, upper-level managers get nervous when something happens, and they don't want to see a repeat of the same situation. In some cases, they become overly cautious and limit a deputy or officer in doing his job because they want to prevent another injury or death. What these managers often forget is that this is a dangerous job. We should learn from other incidents, but we can't cripple our deputies and officers when they try to do their jobs.

    Nevertheless, I dealt with ruminations (reliving the shooting) multiple times a day. Things got worse when I returned to work, but I put on the best face that I could. My command asked me on a daily basis, "How are you doing?" It got to be too much, and eventually I had to tell them that I was fine, and please stop asking. If I needed their support or their help, I would come to them.

    I found that when my team was busy and we had operations, search warrants, surveillance, or community events, that I was focused and could keep my mind off my depression. But when there was downtime, my mind would dive back into my ruminations and thoughts of guilt for not jumping into the apartment when I was shot, and not holding point with Mike at the other apartment so I could quickly supervise the rescue of Ali. None of my team—not even Ali—held me responsible for any of this, and I haven't heard one bad word from anyone in the department either. It was my internal moral gauge that made me feel this way. I was very vocal with my team, and I shared a lot about why I felt this way. I feel like I became even closer to them as a result of my sharing, but it also weakened me as their supervisor.

While my physical wounds had mostly healed, I continued to go deeper into depression. During this time I continued with the ruminations, even with the help of my psychologist and psychiatrist, and I tried more and different medications. In addition to the guilt, major depression, and trouble sleeping, I started to show other signs of post-traumatic stress disorder (PTSD). I began to have more and more nightmares.

Some were about the shooting, but all of the nightmares were about law enforcement scenarios. I would dream about them nightly. I took the sleep medications, but they could be habit forming. At the beginning I took them regularly because I was only getting a couple of hours of sleep a night. Later, I had to cut back because I didn't want to get addicted to the drugs. Still, I wasn't sleeping well.

To this day, good-quality sleep is not something that I get much of, even though I lie in bed for six or eight hours or more. Shortly after getting out of the hospital, I was sleeping so badly that I mixed a few drugs to help me doze off one night. I took a Percocet and an Ambien, and I think I had a beer as well. Well, I woke up in the middle of the night and was hallucinating that the TV was on and that I was seeing things in the room. That freaked out my wife so much that she called Poison Control immediately. The first thing the guy on the phone asked her was, "Has he been shot?" Well, that flipped her out even more. Poison Control said to monitor my breathing and make sure I was fine the next day, which I was.

As time went on, I started having a new sleep issue in addition to the dreams and nightmares: I was talking in my sleep. I've been known to be so deep into nightmares about fights with suspects that I've accidentally hit my wife on a couple of occasions. It was so out of control that my psychiatrist wanted me to take a new medication. I haven't gotten approval through workman's compensation yet. Don't ask me about workman's compensation;

141

I could write a whole other book on that issue alone!

More problems reared their ugly heads: a lack of sex drive, and eating all kinds of fattening foods. I had lost fifteen to twenty pounds from the shooting and subsequent recovery, so I thought I could eat whenever and whatever I wanted to. I gained back the weight I had lost, but I added more pounds to that. I stopped exercising. I didn't feel like going to the gym or getting outside and riding my bicycle or going for a hike. My alcohol intake increased dramatically. I used to drink only on Friday and Saturday nights when Janine and I went to dinner, and even then it was only a couple of drinks. Now I was drinking much more, and I still mixed pain pills on occasion to help me sleep. The alcohol was becoming a crutch for me to deal with the depression. It was one of the few ways I could escape my ruminations, and I found it enjoyable for short periods of time. There is one thing that I never did do, and that was to drive drunk. I was always with my wife, and she was our designated driver every time.

Our sheriff deputies' association hosts an annual dinner and dance for the members. A year after the shooting, the event was held at a local hotel, and I wanted to celebrate. I brought a 750-milliliter bottle of expensive Scotch. I didn't think that bringing my own alcohol would be an issue. So I broke it out and shared with some coworkers before the event got too crowded.

All of a sudden, out of the corner of my eye, I saw a hotel security guard in a suit coming toward us. He was almost running, and he tried to grab my bottle of Scotch, which was on the table.

"Sir," he said, "you can't have that in here. I'm going to have to take it and give it back to you when the dinner is over." I grabbed the bottle from the table before he could. "Back the fuck off," I said.

My wife was right there, and she became our referee to keep me from attacking this guy. It was around this time that, with my alcohol use and depression, I was going through a stage of emotional recovery known as extreme anger. So I was about to blow some steam off on this jerk, who'd gone way overboard, in my mind. I still feel that way. If he had come up to me and said that we couldn't have the Scotch there, I wouldn't have gone off on him. Instead, he stormed in like he was some kind of overzealous security guard.

After my wife calmed me down, I agreed to take the Scotch out to the car and leave it there. Nevertheless, the hotel employee was all over me all night long, trying to act like a tough security guard, I guess. I didn't care. I just drank more alcohol during the event.

Eventually I sneaked my bottle of Scotch back inside and shared it with friends. I didn't understand what the big deal was. I still don't understand why he acted like that. Things kept spinning out of control. I still had some physical issues with my injuries.

As July of 2013 came around, I was a mess! I would sit in my office during quiet times and ruminate about the shooting. I was still having a horrible time sleeping. When I could sleep, all I wanted to do was sleep the day away and not get out of bed. I fell deeper and deeper into depression, and I was suffering more and more from PTSD. I had no motivation to do anything. I could barely get myself out of bed to go to work. I started taking chances with general safety issues. For example, I wasn't concerned if I was shot or injured again. I would also avoid meetings with Sheriff's Command and many other groups—even friends—because I didn't want to deal with any questions. I found that my self-imposed isolation also triggered some paranoia. I believed that people were probably talking about me behind my back, which wasn't necessarily true.

Again, if we had an operation or detail, I could handle it, but during the quiet times my mind wandered back to the shooting. There was some crying and a lot of sadness, mostly at home. I took my sadness and depression to work. Even though I tried to hide it, it still showed, but on a much lower level with my command and my subordinates. However, I did feel that everyone there really cared about me. I understood what I was going through, and that there wasn't any shame in it.

Toward the end of July 2013, I realized that I couldn't do the job right now. What I had gone through was eating me alive. I was trying to keep it together at work, but I wasn't getting better. I was getting worse. I was no longer able to supervise my team effectively, and it showed.

I sat down with my wife to tell her how I felt.

"I'm not well," I said. "I need to go back out on leave."

I knew that this likely meant that I would retire. I wouldn't be coming back. It was time. I had done so much in my career that I was proud of, and I'd received numerous accolades for all that hard work. I was—and still am—very proud of my work ethic and my desire to do the best I could. Hopefully I instilled some of this in the people I worked with, and those who worked for me. Time will tell, I guess.

I pulled out of work to heal and get more help. I was in therapy every week, and I was back on medication to battle my depression, but I was still struggling. Prior to leaving work, at one point I was so angry

I was still struggling. Prior to leaving work, at one point I was so angry after having a bad day at work, I'd gotten on my motorcycle and rode over ninety miles an hour on surface streets—not in an attempt to directly kill myself, but if I was hoping I would crash and die. I had a death wish. I was constantly talking about my death, wishing that someone "would just shoot me." This was a common theme at home, in the way I talked to my wife. I constantly thought about suicide and how I could take my life, but I just couldn't get past the fact that it would devastate Janine. So, as much as I hoped I would die, I wasn't going to do it. But I was deep into the depression and PTSD at that point, and my psychologist knew it and was trying to help me.

What I was putting my wife through, was a shameful thing. She had to put up with my outbursts and try to keep me calm, and she still loved me. She had to put up with my threats of dying, my major mood swings, my anger issues, and everything else. I really put Janine through the wringer, but she stood by me. I must say that, aside from my son, she is the love of my life. Since I don't see my son anymore,

Janine has been my strength, soul, and love, to get me through this. The amount of crap that she's had to deal with in our lives—not just with the shooting, but all of the attempts to get pregnant—it's amazing that she has stayed with me. If not for our faith in God, neither one of us would have survived all that we've been through in the last ten years.

I guess that's why Janine wanted to renew our vows in July of 2012. It had happened a few months before the shooting in September. It was a beautiful ceremony, and we had a wonderful experience with our friends and family.

At one point in my recovery I was still seeing doctors for injuries I had *before* the shooting. I had to go to a doctor, whom I had seen some four years earlier. He was surprised to see me, and even more surprised to hear my story and see my newly added scars. Then he asked me a question:

"If you knew what was going to happen to you, would you still have taken the same career path?"

I wasn't sure what to say to him at the time. I was thinking, *He's an adversarial workman's compensation doctor and is not on my side.* So I didn't really answer.

I thought about it later and the answer is, emphatically, without exception, *Yes!* There is no way that I would want to change my life in any way, just to avoid this or anything else I've been through. It's a ridiculous question in the first place, because that can never happen.

Looking back, though, I wouldn't change anything in my life. Each of our lives is unique. Believing in God and his love, I know that one day I will be there with those I loved and have lost, including our children that we lost, for eternity. No matter what happens here on earth, it will all be wonderful when I get to heaven. I know a lot has happened to my wife and me in this life, but many of these things pale in comparison to some of the experiences of others, so I don't have any room to complain. I just wanted to find a way to deal with the hand that I was dealt, so that I could continue in this life the best way I know how, one day at a time.

CHAPTER 15: Trip to D.C.

In May 2013 our deputy sheriff's association treated Ali, me, and our wives to a trip to National Police Week in Washington, DC. This is a weeklong celebration for law enforcement officers that culminate with a ceremony at the Capitol, honoring law enforcement officers throughout the nation who lost their lives on the job during the previous year. The event can draw up to forty thousand officers from state, local, and federal law enforcement from all over the country and the world.

This was a welcome break for Janine and me. We were able to get away from the routine at work and everything that was troubling me. In addition, the event gave me a perspective that I needed: I was alive, I should try to understand my situation, and I should try to heal. I had a great time with Ali, our wives, other deputies, and many of the directors from the deputy sheriff's association, who came with us and showed us the Capitol. We visited many of the museums, including the Holocaust Museum, the Capitol building, the Spy Museum, Ford's Theatre (where President Lincoln was shot), and the Washington Mall and all the memorials along it.

The culmination of National Police Week consists of two events: a candlelight vigil and a memorial service. The candlelight vigil is held at the National Law Enforcement Officer's Memorial. All of the law enforcement officers present in DC come together at the memorial. There are thousands of cops from all over the country, and many from other countries of the world. I remember seeing officers from Australia and England, for example. There's a memorial service with speakers such as the attorney general, who talk about the risks of the job and the sacrifices that not only we as officers make, but also the sacrifices our families and children have made—especially the sacrifices that are made when an officer is killed in the line of duty.

This really brought it all home for me. It allowed me to celebrate and to remember those who had paid the ultimate price. The service reminded me to be ever so thankful that none of the officers who were present that day had their names engraved on the wall of the memorial. More than nineteen thousand names are currently on that wall. This is where Ali Perez and I coined the phrase, "Not on the Wall," as we shouted it out in praise that we were still alive.

As a law enforcement officer, Ali's well-known explanation of doing his job over the years was that he was "just doing the Lord's work."

The following photos are of the Washington D.C. Law Enforcement Memorial and annual ceremony to remember the officers lost each year.

Det. Carlos L. Ledesma
E.O.W. 07/28/10
THE WICKED FLEE
WHEN NO MAN PURSUETH
BUT THE RIGHTEOUS
ARE BOLD AS A LION
PROVERBS 28:1

The lions at the Law Enforcement Memorial are protecting their cubs, the officers who are named on the wall.

The thin blue line commemorates fallen officers and symbolizes them as protectors of society.

My wife and me in front of the Capitol building.

He used this throughout his career when going on calls. In fact, on that fateful day when we headed out to arrest Witczak, he made the statement to me. "Just doing the Lord's work," he said.

It was the first time I had heard it. It stuck with me. After the shooting, I was looking for inspiration to help me deal with the trauma and violence that I had experienced. I remembered Ali's words, and I decided to get another tattoo. Many of my tattoos are inspirational, and I felt it was time for another one. I looked at images in books and on the Internet. I found a design that featured the Archangel Michael, who, among other things, is the guardian of police officers.

There is a well-known image of Michael, after a battle, holding a spear and stepping on the head of the devil. I believe this comes from the words written in the book of Revelations in the Bible where Michael is triumphant over evil. I thought it apropos to my situation: it was just what I was looking for in an inspirational and fitting tattoo. It now adorns my left calf for everyone to see.

The final part of National Police Week—which, by the way, was started by President John F. Kennedy—occurs at the Capitol building, on the lawn where the president is sworn into office every four years. That year, President Obama (can't stand him) attended the event and personally thanked the family members of fallen officers.

Art work of tattoo on my left calf, by artist Chris Earnhart.

It was a somber and touching ceremony, with thousands of cops from all over the world. Janine and I got some nice photos of us in our dress uniforms. It was unusually hot for May, yet a heavy rain threatened to fall on the Capitol lawn. We were lucky that the heat wasn't too bad, and the rain held off until after the ceremony had ended.

It was definitely the experience of a lifetime, and Janine and I were honored to have been invited.

CHAPTER 16: The Rollercoaster Ride

Coming back from DC, I felt better than I had in a while. My wife felt good too. Although she was a fellow officer, she had a lot to deal with. She was scared for me, and she didn't want me to go back to work. In fact, when she heard about the trip to DC, which originally didn't include her, she didn't want me to go. You see, two days before the shooting, we had seen the police drama *End of Watch*, a movie that starred Jake Gyllenhaal and Michael Peña. The end of that movie was much more dramatic and horrific than our shooting, but it was also similar: the movie portrayed an ambush situation, and we experienced many of the same fears. Of course, *End of Watch* was just a movie. What we experienced was real and had real consequences, which to me means it was worse.

Anyway, Janine told me that she'd had a premonition that something bad was going to happen. When the shooting occurred, it only reinforced her feelings of doom and gloom. As I said, she didn't want me to go back to work. Nor did she want me to go on an airplane without her. She especially didn't want me to take unnecessary risks at my job, which is what I was doing to some extent. She knew that I was a hard charger—that I would get in front of trouble instead of hanging back. This only added to her fears.

I was good at work for a while. However, things still popped up that set me back, and I felt like I was on a rollercoaster ride with some extreme ups and downs. My team was doing some great work that was exciting for me as well. Throughout my career, I've lived off the adrenaline of this job, which can be extremely high at times. Most workdays don't rise to that level, but when they do, watch out!

As I look back at everything that I've been through in my life—not including the shooting—I think I've suffered from depression, to some extent, for many years. How could I not, with all of the loss that I've seen? I think the shooting was the straw that broke the camel's back for me.

I continued to ride this wave of ups and downs. I was probably a little manic-depressive at this point—or, as I think they call it now, bipolar—due to the situation at hand and my depression.

The San Diego Police Department held its awards ceremony before the Sheriff's Department did. S.D.P.D. was going to give the officer who assisted us a Medal of Valor and a Medal of Lifesaving for his actions on that day. I wasn't going to attend; I was still finding reasons not to attend events and to stay out of the media and public eye. I also wanted to avoid people. All of this was related to my PTSD.

However, my command asked me if I would attend the S.D.P.D. ceremony to show respect for the officer and what he'd done during the incident. At first I said no, but then I found out that Ali was going to go, so I felt obligated.

Let me say that the San Diego Police Department is a great agency, even though they've been rocked by a lot of scandal with some of their officers committing crimes. They do a lot without having nearly as much funding and as many officers as my department does. This is due to a lot of politics and people who have tried to make the public servant—with his "outrageous pension"—look like a bad person. I have many friends on the S.D.P.D., and obviously my wife is an officer with them as well. That said there is a rivalry between our agencies to outshine and to give as much crap to each other as is possible, usually in a friendly way. For example, we razz each other about our departments and how much better we are than they are. We give each officer or deputy that kind of "love" when we are blowing off steam and trying to one-up each other. On the other hand, there is within the command structures of both agencies, I believe, an undeniable tendency to make sure that each agency toots its own horn, even if it's without regard for the other agency.

So I went to the S.D.P.D. award ceremony with my wife, my

team, Ali, and his wife. We sat way in the back of the room. Unfortunately, my lieutenant, being the thoughtful person that he is—and I mean that with all respect—strolled to the podium and let the emcee know that we were in the audience. Now the S.D.P.D. wanted Ali and me to get up on stage with this officer when he was awarded his medals.

What you need to understand is that, at the time, I still hadn't put together all of the details about who did what during the rescue. I knew there was animosity on the part of my deputies toward what the media and our department's public affairs unit had portrayed about certain people's actions on that day. It wasn't until more than a year after the incident that I started to get all the facts, and it wasn't until I began writing this book that I discovered all of the inconsistencies about who did what on that day.

So I was extremely upset with my lieutenant, now that he was asking me to go on stage. I didn't want to be paraded up there in any fashion whatsoever! I told him no. Ali, on the other hand, was fine with it. His personal battles stemming from the incident were different than mine, and he was happy to go, for which I applaud him. Me? I didn't want to be there in the first place, let alone get up on the stage. I was steaming mad. This was another PTSD reaction, with almost uncontrollable anger, and I was about to walk out of the venue and go back to work.

Somehow I calmed myself down and agreed to go on stage with Ali. Everyone applauded us, and I listened to what the San Diego Police Department spokesperson had to say about the award they were giving to the S.D.P.D. officer. The S.D.P.D.'s write-up was full of fluff and outright inaccuracies about the facts of that day, and even I could tell. The write-up was so off that it made our department and our deputies look like idiots. Again I started to boil. It took every bit of energy I had to stay on that stage and not storm off.

When the award ceremony was over, I went back to my seat, and I could see that my team was infuriated with what had just happened. I got out of there as fast as I could. I felt down in the dumps again. All the thoughts of my death, and my anger over this incident, came flooding back. I can't remember if I went back to work that afternoon, but I think the next day I called in sick. I know I later told my lieutenant that I was furious with him for what he'd made me do. He apologized. He saw how upset it made me, and he knew that the information the S.D.P.D. put out about the incident was just not true. We all felt it was another "S.D.P.D. moment"—that they were trying to capitalize on something that made them look good in the media.

Since the media had bashed them for so many years, maybe the S.D.P.D. was looking for something to make them look good. That's how I felt at the time.

Later, when I had the full story about the incident, I realized that what S.D.P.D. did made sense. I believe they went off what they believed had happened, and they just didn't know any better. It would have been nice if they had contacted someone at the sheriff's department to verify some of the details, and also to think about how they portrayed us in such a bad light. Oh well. Maybe it's just that competition thing again!

Once again I was on that rollercoaster ride of my life, with extreme ups and downs that just didn't stop. I didn't know how to make it stop. One minute I was fine, and the next I was down and in a deep depression, or screwing things up. I needed to get more help, so back to the doctor's I went.

CHAPTER 17: Trial Preparation—The End is Near

During his time in custody, life got very real for Witczak, and I think he realized that life as he knew it was over. During the first several months of his incarceration he was kept in a "protective custody" housing unit with similar inmates. You get placed in protective custody for a variety of reasons: being a child molester, a high-profile criminal, or a gang member, for example. All of these prisoners are considered to be in protective custody because someone could hurt them. If the inmate is a gang member, then a member from a rival gang may want to hurt him. Obviously, child molesters are in danger because so many of the inmates were molested as children themselves. Child molesters are usually housed in the same module as gang members, with a common day room, but they are also supposed to be kept separate from others in protective custody, such as gang members, to prevent attacks on them.

Well, something happened when Witczak was in the day room making a phone call by himself. Apparently the deputies working in the module didn't realize that Witczak was still on the phone; there was a blind spot that made it difficult to see the inmate. Another inmate—whom I knew very well when I worked in Vista, and whom I "lost my cherry" to, on my first stolen vehicle pursuit—was let out for his turn to use the phone. This inmate was a member of the Vista Homeboy Gang (VHB). He was probably in his thirties by now, had been arrested numerous times, and was facing two life terms on attempted murder charges. He had joined the big-time affiliate prison gang known as the Mexican Mafia (EME). So when he got out of his cell, he made a beeline for Witczak. I'm sure he knew that Witczak had been arrested for child molestation and possibly for the attack on my team and me.

The VHB inmate pummeled Witczak with his fists and did some serious damage to Witczak's face. Witczak tried to cover up as the VHB inmate dragged him across the day room module floor and completely out of his jail-issued pants. The VHB inmate continued to pummel Witczak until deputies finally got to him and stopped the fight. When he saw deputies arriving, the VHB inmate headed back to his cell. Witczak was able to reach the door of the module, where deputies rescued him. He suffered multiple contusions to his head and face, and some of the strikes slashed the side of his face as if he had been cut by a knife. The incident was caught on video surveillance, and I observed the fight on video at a later date.

Witczak never had a chance. He was victimized so innocently, just like he'd victimized those poor little girls. The fact that the inmate who attacked him was an old foe of mine when I worked the streets of Vista was sort of funny to me. Of course, I doubt the inmate knew who I was; this was his taking vengeance on Witczak for what he'd done. It may have also been a way for the VHB inmate to make himself look good, now that he was a member of the Mexican Mafia. Nevertheless, I did smile a little when I saw the video—just a little!

Deputies tried to convince Witczak to go into Administrative Segregation (Ad Seg), where he would be alone and safe, but he refused, even after the first attack. I think Witczak didn't care what happened to him, nor did he want the complete and utter isolation that is Ad Seg. He'd face Ad Seg anyway, once he got to prison.

Witczak's problems in the module weren't over. A second inmate attacked him with a jail knife known as a "shank." *Shank* is an old-school prison term used to describe the metal support piece in the bottom of dress shoes back in the forties and fifties. Inmates will make shanks out of anything they can get their hands on. Since all they have is time, they come up with all kinds of ways to get in trouble. Shanks are no longer allowed in jail shoes. I've seen shanks made of metal—for example, ground-down silverware that was stolen from the jail kitchen—and inmates will also tear pieces of metal from the walls to grind down into shanks. Another way to make a shank is from one or more toothbrushes. If the inmate can smuggle in a lighter or matches, he or she can melt the toothbrushes together and grind them down to create an effective stabbing tool.

Unfortunately I don't have all the information on the second attack, and it wasn't caught on video like the first one. I did see Witczak's face after the attack, during his preliminary hearing, and the attacker had cut him severely. The cut started under Witczak's neck, traveled all the way across, and up the right side of his face. This could have been a life-threatening injury if the attacker had cut just a little deeper. The size and depth of the wounds, and the scar that was left behind, were very large. Witczak wouldn't be able to hide them, or so I thought.

Once again, Witczak had survived an attack. The jail staff wasn't going to let him take any more chances with his life. They moved him into Ad Seg until his visit at the jail was completed and he was sent to prison. He became belligerent with jail staff and tried to tear off some metal to make his own shank, probably to defend himself. (This is why most inmates make shanks.)

During the preliminary hearing, Witczak refused to go to the courthouse. Deputies had to lift him into a wheelchair to get him into the courtroom. I think he knew his life was over, and he just didn't care. He wasn't going to make it easy for anyone to put him in prison. It was his last act of defiance.

None of the suspects were prosecuted for attacking Witczak, primarily because he refused to cooperate and wasn't willing to prosecute any of them. I'm sure that deputies may have been disciplined for the attacks that occurred, and for that I am truly sorry. I know there was no love for Witczak from our fellow deputies because of what he did to us, but I don't believe any of the attacks occurred because of action taken by the deputies.

During the preliminary hearing, which determines if the defendant can be held accountable for the charges, Ali, Mike, and I did not want to have to relive the experience that we had been through. We didn't want to be seen in the media, and we tried to avoid the media circus at all costs. We came in through a back door to the courthouse, out of the public and the eye of the media. We sat in the back of a jury room, waiting to be called to the stand. Mike was really nervous, and I was as well. I asked Ali if he was going to tell the court about his experience with Jesus during the shootout. He said he was, and I was so proud of him for being willing to testify to the greatness of God's presence in his life on that fateful day.

Ali was the first to be called to testify. Sure enough, he relived the whole incident about meeting Jesus in a chair, and the floating letter that Jesus sent down to Ali, telling him to bless Witczak.

I was next, and I was able to keep it together and testify in a professional manner. It was easier than I thought it would be. One thing I'll always remember is seeing Witczak for the first time in person. I'd never met him, and I never saw him on the day of the incident. He had the huge scar on his face from where he was cut by the shank. He had shaved his head, and he must have done it himself, because he looked ridiculous. He had one tuft of hair coming out the left side of his head, and the hair was probably three inches long. It was a clump of hair—enough to grab with your fist. It reminded me of those babies that are deformed, with another head attached to theirs. It just looked bizarre!

That night after court, the big story on the news was Ali's testimony about seeing Jesus. It was on every TV channel and in every newspaper, and I was proud of him for taking a stand and witnessing about his interaction with Jesus. Most everyone I knew had nothing but positive things to say about both our testimonies. Mike never had to testify, and I think he was relieved about that. It was pointless to make all three of us relive the event, but we had no control over that.

In the end, though, I think it was a good thing, because Ali was able to give his statement, which had great impact throughout the community. Some people, I'm sure, doubt his story, but that doesn't matter to me. It gave me strength to know that when Ali was in his darkest hour, God was there for him. For a long time, I didn't understand where God was when *I* was shot. I knew that He was there, but the pain and guilt I felt were strangling me. I felt as if God hadn't helped me to deal with my issues like he had helped Ali.

Just after the one-year anniversary of the incident, and after getting back from a vacation to New York City to see the 9/11 Memorial and other historic sites, I prepared for the trial against Witczak. I had been dreading this for the entire year. Witczak had become despondent in custody and refused to take a plea deal (plead guilty), even though the prosecutor had a slam-dunk case on our attempted murder, as well as the molestation of the two girls.

Each of us—Ali, Mike, and I—had to sit down with the district attorney (DA) and review the statements that we had made over a year ago. I would finally see the evidence in the case. I had never seen the crime scene photos or the damage to my TAC vest.

At our meeting with the DA, he showed me all the photos of

the entire scene, from aerial photos of the apartment complex, to the inside of Witczak's apartment, to the apartment where Mike and I had taken shelter. I got to see all of it. I'd already seen Deputy Hammers' lapel video, and that was going to be included as evidence, if necessary. I got to see where Ali's and my blood spilled on the landing and in both apartments as well. I think the most shocking thing for me was seeing the amount of blood on the stairs where they had dragged Ali to safety. There was so much of it.

The most significant and enlightening thing for me was seeing the pictures where the rounds had exited the building in my direction. For a long time I thought that I'd been hit with three rounds. I thought the first round hit my left arm, the second one hit my left side, and the third hit my right side. I later realized that the bruise on my right side turned out to be from Mike's boot when he kicked in the door so we could take cover. There were gaps in my memory as to what occurred and when. By reviewing the crime scene, some things started to make more sense.

To the right of the apartment door, near the door trim of Witczak's apartment, there was a bullet exit hole that went straight down the landing toward where we were standing. The bullet hole was at about the height of what had hit me in the side, and was right by the door to the apartment. I believe what happened is that the round Witczak fired pierced the wood and the drywall and the stucco and had decelerated and fragmented. This explained the wood fragments in my left leg. I believe one round splintered the wood into my pants, and then into my legs.

    The same bullet continued and hit my arm and split it open like a potato, from the middle of my forearm to the rear of my elbow. I believe that fragments continued into my TAC vest on my side, penetrated it, and went into my chest cavity between my ribs. Finally, another fragment from the same bullet penetrated my upper chest area after going through the vest and my left breast. From what I recall, coupled with the location of my wounds and the trajectory of the bullets, I believe I was facing the kitchen window to cover Mike S. and Ali from the rear of the group, since Mike S. was between Ali and me.

    This made sense because the wounds all came through my left side, which was closest to the door when I was facing the window. Mike S. later told me he felt and could see a bullet fly by him. This was probably the bullet that hit me. It is possible that Mike, filled with adrenaline, could have seen this, it's been documented in other incidents before.

I realized that had the bullet not traveled through the wall and wood, the velocity of the fragment that hit me in the breast by my heart would have traveled through my heart and/or my lungs, and I would not be here today. I realized how much God was looking out for me on that day, and it gave me some relief and help with my PTSD and depression. I just wished that I could have seen all of this evidence a long time ago, so that it didn't have to take over a year for me to figure all this out!

Several months later, I finally got my TAC vest back. The department released it to me to keep and use as a training tool for future recruits and anyone else who wanted to listen and learn. When I first saw my vest, it was covered in light-colored, gunk-like flakes. I believe the flakes were remnants of my arm that were blasted onto the TAC vest after I was shot. Looking closer, I saw that there were more brass fragments on the inside and outside of the vest. One fragment had penetrated the vest cover and stopped where the fabric holds the ballistic material. The fragment had partially pinned itself to the fabric. It was an even larger fragment than the one that I had taken out of my breast.

I examined the entry points for the two fragments that went into my chest cavity, and the one that landed on my breast. Both entries on the ballistic vest—also known as "failure points"—were on my left side, at the edge of the ballistic vest panels that wrap around the body. In fact, the failure points were at the edge of—and less than an inch from—the edge of the material. Apparently, none of the material from the back panel of the ballistic material overlapped the front panel, which would have given me some extra protection, but may not have stopped the bullet. This is probably because I was heavier and the vest didn't overlap each side, or I could have been moving to the point that the material stretched away from the sides. I thought I had enough material overlapping, as I was already aware of this issue, but apparently I did not. This is something that other officers should keep in mind when they're being fitted for a new vest.

So the trial date had been set, and the prosecution was ready to go with the case. The trial was expected to take about a week, maybe a week and half at most. Suddenly, out of nowhere, Witczak told his attorney that he was willing to take a plea and end this. We waited for the court hearing. The plan was to allow Witczak to plead guilty, be sentenced immediately, and sign a waiver for any and all appeals, if he was willing to do so. Normally this would play out over several months with a guilty plea, followed months later with sentencing and the victim's impact statements. No one was sure if Witczak was really going to take the plea, so the DA wanted to combine the plea and sentencing. It was a foregone conclusion that he would already know what he was being sentenced to, when it was handed down by the judge. Witczak was sentenced to a complicated amount of time. In essence, he was given life in prison, and will not have a chance for parole before he dies there. When Ali and I gave our victim impact statements, we were allowed to speak to Witczak, who looked away from us. He had grown a full beard that covered up the scars on his face and neck. Here is what I told him on that day:

> Daniel, I want to take you back to that day on September 25, 2012. The reason I want to do this is because every day since then, I relive that day in my head. I wish I could get those nightmares out of my head, but I just can't seem to do that right now. I hope that one day the memories of that horrific day will fade or go away all together. Only time will tell for me. I wonder about you. Do you think about what you did on that day, and the subsequent days before that day? I guess you will have the rest of your life to think about it, while you waste away in prison.

You know you caused great bodily injury to me and Detective Perez, let alone the fact that you were trying to kill us. You also caused great emotional injury not only to us, but other deputies who were there, and even more importantly to the two girls whom you sexually assaulted. Regardless of our injuries, what you did to those girls is unspeakable, and you will have to live with that for the rest of your life. I pray to God that they will not remember what happened to them, so that they won't have to live with the memories of the violence and despicable acts that you did to them.

As deputies, we get paid to do this job, and we do it knowing that one day we may have to give our lives to protect the citizens we serve. None of us do this job lightly, with disregard for our lives and the lives of our partners. We don't go to work expecting that this will be our last day on earth, our last day with our friends, and most importantly our last day with our families. What you did on that day was try to take our lives, and take us away from all of that—all that we hold dear in our lives.

You shortened the careers of three deputy sheriffs on that day. You took the innocence of two young girls on that day. You caused me and my family great pain and suffering. You caused Detective Perez's family even greater pain and suffering. Although you tried to end our lives on that day, you failed. In fact, with all the heartache and pain that my family and I live with to this day, there have been some great things that came from this incident. Thanks to your disregard for the lives of all involved in this tragedy, Jesus Christ presented himself to Detective Perez in his hour of need. Because of his faith in God, Jesus sent him a message to forgive you and to bless you. Detective Perez did that on that day, and I truly believe that changed the outcome of your actions and future actions that you could have taken on that day. For that I'm eternally grateful—not to you, but to God through Jesus Christ!

So, as a Christian, I will take the high road for these last few words. I still remember bleeding from the wounds you inflicted on me on that day, trying to find cover from your high-powered rifle that reached out to me through the walls of your apartment. At that time, we were shooting back at you, and we finally paused. I thought that I should call out to you. I really wanted to try and talk to you on that day, to reason with you and get you to give up. I didn't, because I was terrified that if I tried to talk some sense into you, that you would become aggravated and then kill Detective Perez. So on that day, I didn't do it.

On this day, though, I will. I will tell you that I have forgiven you, as a Christian. Christ has forgiven me for my sins, and I forgive you for yours. I hope that you will listen to the words of Christ. You should take a moment and heed these words! You will have the rest of your life to think about what you've done. Why not read the Bible? Why not listen to the words of Jesus, and find God while you sit in prison for the rest of your life? You still have a chance at redeeming your life, but it's up to you, as it is for all of us. If you do, and you repent your sins, you can be forgiven, and you can find a way through Christ for eternal life.

In John, verses 3 through 16, it talks about how God so loved the world that He gave his only son, so that everyone who has faith in Jesus will have eternal life. God sent Jesus to save us, not to condemn us. As Jesus was hung on the cross, beside him there were two thieves who were also hung on the cross. As Jesus explained to both that they could be saved through him, one of them took him up on it. Jesus told him he would meet him in paradise because of it. It's never too late for you, Daniel, and I hope God will bless you one day as well!

Daniel Witczak never looked at either Ali or me, and he never had anything to say about being sorry for what he had done. I can only hope that, maybe, I reached him with my words, but I'll probably never know.

CHAPTER 18: Doctor, Doctor, Give me the Cure!

As I've mentioned, throughout this ordeal, I sought help from counselors, including a psychologist and eventually a psychiatrist. I also took medication for depression to raise my serotonin, endorphin, and dopamine levels, which control the brain's ability for a person to be happy. There are too many drugs to talk about, and each works differently on an individual, so I won't discuss this in depth except to say that I did find some help with these medications.

The bulk of the help came from a psychologist whom I have seen regularly since the shooting. Initially, I dealt with things in stages, very similar to the stages someone deals with when a loved one passes away. I had issues in these areas, most notably with the stage of guilt and grief. In addition, the biggest hurdle I had to overcome—and I have been successful with—is the stage of anger.

My anger took hold of me in many ways and under many circumstances that I've described in previous chapters. I was finally able to let go of it, and it is now under control like any "normal" person. If I hadn't been able to get my anger under control, it would have been the death of me. With the anger and excessive drinking, which is also under control, I would have continued to spiral down that slippery slope, with no way back. I'm extremely grateful to have this part of my life back.

    After my initial healing was progressing, I sought help for all of the things that I've discussed. My psychologist helped me through many of the darkest times in my life, and taught me some things to deal with the many issues I had and, to some extent, still have. Some of the techniques that he used were tools that any psychologist or psychiatrist might use on any patients; they aren't a secret. These tools helped me and others who were there on that day, and I'm sure they have helped hundreds of other law enforcement officers and military personnel who have experienced similar events.

    Most of my therapy involved talking about the incident, my feelings, and my fears. Doing this frequently, with a professional, helped me control my emotions and thoughts that were tied to the trauma. It helped to have someone to listen to me who was not involved in the incident. That someone was also not a family member whom I would burden with more stress as he or she listened to how I was feeling and how I was learning to cope with the intensity of the trauma. In fact, my wife came along on a couple of visits, and sought her own counseling for issues that she felt more comfortable sharing with someone else.

    My goal was to find a way to regulate the reaction to the stress in my life. I used stress-reduction techniques to help me find a way to lower my stress and my physiological indicators such as heart rate and blood pressure. Exercise was also a key ingredient in raising the levels of chemicals in the brain that help to make you feel better—it's a big factor.

My treatment also included having an awareness of my issues and tools to calm myself, and to learn how to do it on my own. It's a funny thing that one of these tools is called the "continuous calm exposure technique"! This was done by putting me into a sort of meditative state where I controlled my breathing, focused on my thoughts, and tried to put myself mentally in a place where I could remember being happy. I used not only the visualization of being in the place, but also the sounds and smells associated with that place. The actions of controlled breathing and changing my thoughts to a "happy place" helped to calm me down and take me out of the thoughts that were painful. I was trained to do this in the office with the psychologist, and also when I was on my own and things came up in the real world.

Another technique that is widely used with military and law enforcement personnel following a traumatic event is called EMDR, or Eye Movement Desensitization and Reprocessing. The goal of EMDR, as I understand it, is to learn to process traumatic events and memories that remain unresolved. The goal is to reduce their lingering effects to help the person find a way to cope, and to find a mechanism to do so. From what I know of EMDR, it requires a trained professional to do it with you each and every time. I didn't use EMDR, as my psychologist preferred other techniques that were similar and obtained the same results that I could use on my own.

    I don't claim to be an expert, but what I can say is that I believe these tools helped me to process the memories and dreams to a certain extent, and helped me find a way to control my anger with regard to the lingering effects from the shooting. My doctors also used Cognitive Behavioral Therapy (CBT), which helped me to understand why I had certain thoughts and feelings. CBT helped me realize that all of those thoughts and feelings were normal for what I had gone through. The bottom line? All of it definitely helped me, and has continued to help me. It's the reason I'm sharing my thoughts and feelings about this incident with you. If one person finds that this discussion helped him or her to deal with a traumatic event in life, and knows that others went through the same types of things, it may help someone to seek help, as I did.

    While I was writing this book, I saw something on Facebook

from a group called "Surviving the Shield." It was a saying that summed up how we have to deal with things in our lives. Some experiences may be like mine, and others may be worse, but all are significant. The saying goes like this:

*You can always take the easy way out and give up, but Real Strength comes when you **decide** to keep pushing forward no matter what the circumstances are.*

Just like the letter that the sixth-grader Rocio, wrote to me, I had tunnels to go through, and I was very much in a tunnel at times. I didn't see a way out, and I've had to work hard to find it. I can see the end of the tunnel now. I feel better about where I came from and where I am going. The only thing that I don't know is where I am going. The career I had for almost a quarter century is one that is very difficult. It's stressful, and it's not a job for everyone. Since doing this job, though, I know that I will never have another like it. I will not be able to replicate the exhilaration of this career, and it will be hard for me to feel the same way about another job ever again, but I will try.

Maybe that's the point, though: I always wanted to be in the line of fire, so to speak—always wanting to play the game—and at some point, I didn't know how to slow down or stop. It's obvious to me now that I need to move into another career, maybe still in the law enforcement realm. I don't know, but I'll figure it out with the help of my faith, family, and friends. So maybe this is God's way of showing me that I need to move on, keep the memories and great friends that I've made over the years, and move to something less demanding, both physically and mentally.

 Throughout this ordeal and my life since the shooting, I've put my faith and trust in God that He will show me the way to my future. I will continue to do that for the rest of my life. I wrote this book as a therapeutic tool to help me heal from this incident and to put it into perspective. I also wanted to help anyone who has, or is going through, similar experiences, to know that they are not alone and they can find help too. Suicide is not the answer. It will only devastate your family and friends and make their hearts ache for you. If you take that action, it may lead others onto that wrongful route in coping with overwhelming feelings. It solves nothing! I only hope that I have reached someone by writing this book.

CHAPTER 19: The Thin Blue Line

I completed this book in 2014, but decided not to publish it. I was concerned the personal details of my life were too much for me to disclose to the public. I changed my mind at the end of 2014 for reasons I will explain shortly.

I am very proud of the work I did in law enforcement. I am very proud of the people who I worked with and the high caliber professionalism they displayed. I'm proud that I helped citizens both directly, and the community indirectly by arresting people who were out to commit crimes that hurt both. I believe each of us in law enforcement starts this career to make a difference. As we enter the beginning of our career we know there will be exciting and crazy experiences. We realize later as our time in the field progresses that the exciting and crazy moments are few and far between. There are many who start this career who do not last long for a variety of reasons. Some cannot do this job that requires multi-tasking complex duties and quick decision making. Others leave as a result of things seen during a law enforcement career such as violent crimes, murders, suicides, deaths, and tragedies involving children. Those who continue with a law enforcement career continue to make a difference every day with little or no public appreciation.

Occasionally they are recognized by the department they work for and even more rarely by the public they serve. Yet they do not do it for the recognition. They do the job to the best of their abilities, because it is the right thing to do. The men and women in law enforcement have a high moral compass that guides them to do the job correctly, and the way the public wants and demands that do, for the most part. They serve and protect the public each and every day.

Yes, in many locales they get paid fairly well compared to some professions. In some communities they receive a pension for the rest of their lives if they live long enough to retire. However, at what cost?

The things men and women in law enforcement must do and live with for the rest of their lives are often very damaging to their personal lives and their careers. In addition, it is estimated that every 53 hours, a law enforcement officer is killed in the line of duty. Let alone the tens of thousands of assaults that officers are the victims of. Ask yourself if you were to do the job, would you put up with all that law enforcement has to deal with that include small things such as people hating you for your profession, being scrutinized for every little thing in the public eye, and having parents tell their kids to be good children or the police will arrest them. Or imagine dealing with the bigger things such as being spat on for doing your job, being attacked physically by a drunk idiot who does not care about you or themselves, being stabbed or cut with a knife by an assailant during a violent confrontation on a domestic violence call. Imagine being shot at or shot while trying to stop the robbery of a local convenience store. Imagine being subjected to all of these things just because you are doing the job. The job you love regardless of all these things. The only job you would want to do, because it is the most challenging yet rewarding job you will ever have. Imagine what our country would be like if no one did this job. Our country would be in chaos.

Recent events around the country involving protests of suspected police brutality propel a belief that law enforcement is out of control with excessive use of force. There is a belief that police are murdering innocent people just because of the color of their skin, and a call for police to be murdered just because of the job they do. I have become overwhelmed with a deep sadness of these beliefs by some misguided people who do not have a clue as to what law enforcement does. They lack understanding of what we do every day to protect the citizens of our communities. I am overwhelmed with the anger directed at law enforcement at the perception of things we do wrong. I believe most law enforcement officers have never done what the public believe is a wrongful or criminal act of using force to affect an arrest; or in the most unfortunate of circumstances, having to take a life.

What people do not seem to understand is if we did not do this job what would be the reality of a country without law enforcement keeping the peace? When law enforcement officers first started in this country we were not known as "Cops," Police Officers, or Deputy Sheriffs; we were known as "Peace Officers." A Peace Officer in reality is what law enforcement really is. They keep the peace in our communities. They resolve numerous disputes without ever having to arrest anyone. They work with each other every day to keep the peace and to hold that "Thin Blue Line." That line is the peace keepers putting their lives on the line every day for the benefit of the community they serve and live in, to preserve the lives and the country we know and love.

Tyranny and havoc would rein down on this country without this thin blue line. Just take a look at some of the various countries in the world where law enforcement no longer can do their job. There is unspeakable violence, rapes, robberies, beheadings, and murders for no reason other than to create tyranny and violent take overs of these places, often in the name of religion.

I became so disgusted with all of the outrage against law

enforcement recently that I felt compelled again to speak out about my career, my life, and the profession I loved so much. The career I sacrificed so much for all in the name of keeping the peace. I hope one day cooler heads will prevail in this country and the sobering reality of what all of us in law enforcement do every day for everyone in our communities will be realized. The Peace Keepers will always, "hold the thin blue line" even for those who hate the profession.

For law enforcement presentations or any other need, you can contact Craig Johnson at: shots_fired_deputy_down@yahoo.com